The Matapaua Conversations

The Matapaua Conversations

Peter Calvert & Keith Hill

attar‖books

Contents

Introduction

I have long been fascinated by the big questions: How did the universe begin? Of what is reality constituted? What is the nature of consciousness? What is the relationship between the spiritual and the physical? How does a soul connect with a body? Why are we here? What is the purpose of it all?

Over the aeons human beings have answered these questions using ideas, images and metaphors that made sense to them in the context of the times in which they lived. Zoroaster, Moses, Buddha, Pythagoras, Lao Tzu, Socrates, Jesus, Mohammed, and the sages who wrote the Upanishads each formulated answers to the big questions using language and ideas current during their eras. Today we naturally consider the big questions in the context of our own cultural outlook. We can't do otherwise.

For me, given that I live in twenty-first century New Zealand, the context is secular, liberal and multicultural. My birth coincided with the beginning of the space age, so scientific discoveries naturally dominate my cultural outlook. I attended Protestant Sunday School as a child, where I learned ancient Jewish stories and Christian doctrines. But my tenuous connection to organised religion ceased at the age of thirteen. As a result, I entered my teenage years with no affiliation or obligation to any ideology, whether religious, scientific or political.

Being curious about the world, I used my freedom to explore many different scientific, religious and spiritual ideas, following whatever interested me at the time. My enquiry ranged across world religions, cultural histories and Eastern and Western spiritual traditions. Among the sciences, I was particularly drawn to cosmology, relativity, quantum physics, psychology, and evolution as it applies to biology, culture and the social sciences.

This study made a number of things clear. One is that as humanity learns new facts about the world, previous explanations inevitably become obsolete. While many people remain attached to ancient religious texts and doctrines, for us today scientific explanations have superseded mythological and religious metaphysical explanations. But even scientific understanding needs to be updated in the light of new discoveries. The truths of Newtonian physics were revealed as partial by relativity and quantum physics. In the end the search for knowledge, wisdom and truth has no end. There is always more to know.

Answers to the big questions can be no different. As times change perceptions alter, old truths are replaced by new truths, and the big answers need to be updated using terminology, analogies, symbols and metaphors that make sense in the context of current understanding of the world. This is especially required in the twenty-first century because human knowledge has increased exponentially over the last one hundred years. The result is that while many of the ancient big answers to the big questions remain suggestive, and can be kept relevant by reinterpreting them in the light of present knowledge, what we really need are new answers to the big questions that speak directly to us today.

That is what this book is all about. It has risen from a desire to come to a spiritual view of existence in relation to current scientific knowledge.

This brings me to my collaborator, Peter Calvert.

Peter is a meditator and channeller of spiritual literature emanating from non-embodied beings. I initially met him at a book fair in 2008 where he presented his first book, *Agapé and the Hierarchy of Love*.

The truth is I had always avoided channelled books. While I was widely read in all other genres of spiritual writing, I had assumed that there was something suspect about channelled literature, that it was unreliable. So I had never read any channelled books at all.

However, after reading *Agapé* I not only changed my mind, I offered to help edit and publish Peter's second channelled book, *Guided Healing*. I was drawn in by the ideas expressed in both books. But I was also attracted by the voice that came through Peter. It was knowledgeable, no nonsense, possessed intellectual nuance, was spoken from a height above the human, and presented an impartial overview of human existence. It seemed reasonable. And it made sense to me. If this material had come from a human being I would have wanted to ask more. The fact that it came from a supposedly non-embodied source did not diminish the value of the content. Or the intrigue. Furthermore, a little research revealed that there is a growing body of channelled literature published in the last fifty years generated by other supposed non-embodied beings.

Who are they? What are their motives? Do they really speak to us through Peter and others? Or are channellers self-deluded shysters who are lying to get attention, make money, or whatever? Readers will have to make up their own mind regarding the source and validity of the material presented here. I personally tend to be sceptical of expansive claims. However, I suggest the following be considered.

If we accept that human beings are spiritual identities who continue to exist after the animal body dies (or, at least, if we are willing to assume this for the sake of exploration), then it is possible that those living in a non-embodied spiritual state could make contact with us on Earth and offer advice and guidance. Just as adults have love for children and naturally wish to nurture, teach and guide them as they grow, so it is not outlandish to consider that the spiritually mature, having lived their own lives on Earth, and continuing now to exist in a non-embodied state, out of loving concern would wish to nurture, teach and guide us as we strive to best live our lives. In this context it is understandable that such beings would offer, through individuals capable of channelling their communications, written statements regarding the human condition.

This, in fact, is the stated purpose of the non-embodied beings who speak in these pages. Simply, they are beings who were once human, who dwell now in what comes next, and who are looking back at us as we struggle to understand ourselves and the world. Their motive is to illuminate and help.

But there was another reason I was intrigued by Peter's ability to channel. This was that it offered a huge opportunity to further explore the big questions. After all, if you had access to non-embodied beings, wouldn't you want to ask them how reality looks to them from "up there"? So I saw this as a chance to discover their thoughts on the origin of the universe, the nature of reality, how the spiritual connects to the physical, what consciousness is, and so on. If they wouldn't answer, or if their answers failed to convince, what would be lost in the asking? Only the time it took to formulate the questions. On the other hand, if they answered seriously, there was potentially much to learn.

Accordingly, I asked Peter if he would, on my behalf, seek answers to some of the questions that had long intrigued me. He said he was happy to do so, but he needed to ask the non-embodied beings if they were willing to take part. Their response was yes. So I spent three months conceiving an initial list of sixty-six questions.

Several weeks after I gave Peter the questions he went away on a retreat, staying alone in a summer house on a beach in Matapaua, on New Zealand's Coromandel Peninsula. He ended up doing four short retreats between 24 April and 25 September, 2012.

The answers to the questions were spoken through Peter. He recorded his voice, then transcribed the recording and double-checked it for accuracy. I subsequently edited Peter's transcripts for readability. In the process I eliminated a number of questions because they were redundant. I also joined some answers as they read better that way. However, the content of the responses was not altered.

I generated the second list of questions (what became 54 to 100 here) after editing and processing the first set of responses. These questions picked up on the terminology and concepts presented in the first phase of responses.

As it turned out the questions I asked stimulated responses that went way beyond what either Peter or I expected. Some responses provide highly detailed and direct answers. Other responses slide past the questions. Others ignore the questions altogether, on the grounds that the questions are confused, irrelevant or reflect a human view that is invalid from a non-embodied perspective. However, I am very happy that even my most naive questions stimulated such cohesive, wide-ranging and deeply considered responses.

While the non-embodied beings maintain that their responses here consist merely of updated formulations of ancient concepts, there is certainly much that reads as new. Using language and concepts drawn from the sciences, *The Matapaua Conversations* presents a striking view of reality, spirituality and the human situation. We offer it to you to make of as you will.

Keith Hill

22 October, 2012

A note on presentation: The diary Peter kept during the retreats is presented in serif font, *Keith's questions and comments are in serif italics.* **Responses made by the**

CHAPTER ONE

Preparation

26 April 2012

I have arrived at the house at Matapaua where I'll be spending the next few days. I've set up my laptop, ergonomic keyboard and a 4GB USB memory stick for storing files. Surprisingly, I do not feel hungry yet, even though I have had neither breakfast nor lunch and spent about three hours this morning painting the final coat on the back wall of my flat. So my body is a bit sore in places, particularly my neck. I'll need an early night.

The beach is occupied by only a few birds. No one else seems to be in residence here. The weather is intermittent rain from a moist north-easterly, so it is warmer than what I have prepared for. No doubt that will change.

I forgot to bring eggs and coffee, but otherwise have plenty of food. I recently watched a television program that showed drinking coffee induced a forty per cent reduction of the brain's blood flow. That's a worry! So perhaps I'll drink something else as well while I'm here.

I have designated this retreat as an opportunity for those I consult at such times to answer Keith's questions. Keith texted me today to express his appreciation for my undertaking this retreat for his benefit. His questions will exercise all my capacity, I think, given their scope. But, after reading them through initially some weeks ago, I have already had internal confirmation that they will all be answered. We will see. I've also brought my art set, so if any imagery arises I have tools by which to portray it.

27 April

I slept after breakfast and was woken by a sudden chill signal, so have risen to write as requested. Inside me the sound of tinnitus (energy?) in my ears is loud now. I feel calmer than yesterday, but not yet fully rested.

It will be three more days before we can depart this Earth together for an introduction to the skies and beyond. Get oil and coffee to sustain you in the ways you prefer. That is all.

I drove to Kuaotunu for cooking oil, coffee and milk. A feature of my stay so far has been awareness to an unusual degree of the small fears, anxieties and old injunctions concerning safe navigation, such as walking around in hazardous territory like paths, and watching for rocks that may be slippery with moisture and slime. I seem to have greater awareness than normal of a deep layer of early experience in which my parents, or some other caregivers, gave me these kinds of verbal messages. Or else I experienced such things myself.

A small amount of debris has washed up on the shore, including plastic pellets and noodle food sachets. Presumably they're from the Rena shipwreck. I saw a young black-backed gull attempting to eat the contents of one sachet. I'm tired now. Will sleep again.

18:06. Woke with a train of thought that led to the idea that the emergency call sign SOS (... _ _ _ ... = Save Our Souls) is fundamentally inappropriate, as souls are never in significant danger, so do not need saving. It is obvious to me that the thrall of Christianity has been such as to yoke the myth of soul loss to the idea that to save a person is to save their soul, a task self-ascribed to Christianity, which invented the myth in the first place!

Not quite true, but sufficient for the argument to have impact.

Then how did the myth arise originally?

The most ancient cave dwellings show the impact of experience acquired in trance, when the populace did not know of their destination at death. A primitive, inexperienced soul does not know where to go and has to be led away at death. That means that any living population has a co-population of lingering spirits.

There have always been those who act as shamans, who have been instructed in procedures to care for the local community, including the remnant of lingering dead. Variations of perception among shamans, multiplied by their dependence on different preexisting beliefs, has led to a range of interpretations of the experience they acquired during the process of initiating interventions intended to lead individuals to the clear light after their death.

Simplified and condensed versions of such experiences have been averaged across time and within languages and cultures to create variations of the death myth, including stories of its horrors – for everyone loves a ghost tale and its exaggerations. So the death myth became replete with tests and tasks that impede the journey home, when in fact for almost everyone it is a simple task, easily accomplished.

Christians, and others before them, drew on the material at hand to create a specific religious form of the myth, which they then used to enhance their own capture rate of the living. When that is systematically taught to the young, the task of indoctrination is easy.

This is sufficient to account for the success of Christianity as a religion on the world stage. It does not make their version of the death myth any truer than any other historically propagated version, for all are wrong, because they are all exaggerated.

It is only now, since the systematic destruction of religion by science, that a fresh start may be made in the straightforward description of what happens to most people at death. That is our task, to be achieved via the transmission of this teaching.

28 April

I have slept well and long. My body feels rested again. Yet feeling heavy now with input. I will go to my stool to talk into the dictaphone.

We come to begin the developmental and systematic aspects of this teaching, fostered and communicated by the man Keith Hill. Given that it is at his request that we respond to his questions, we feel that proper acknowledgement should be made to the facilitative agreement that he has with us and with you. This agreement was made pre-life, of course.

When contemplating engagement with the earthly realm, you both felt there was an opportunity to contribute to a deeper understanding of the human condition. The opportunity was undertaken in a spirit of self-exploration and self-development. It also involved community engagement and company-inspired social development – "company" in this sense is to be interpreted as meaning a social group whose members share a curiosity concerning the dynamics of life and existence. That is the basis on which you associate with each other, to the somewhat tenuous degree that you do, each uncertain as to the real intention, yet individually committed to the self-chosen developmental path on which you each have embarked, as those paths can now be understood.

We speak in this way at the beginning of the transition into yet deeper states by this one through whom we currently communicate. And we would remark on our input to the man Keith Hill, for he has come to know us well. The combination of two distinct individuals, each driven by a transitory impulse towards self-development (transitory in this instance meaning for the duration of one lifetime), is to work together for mutual individual and group purpose. The group in question is the spectrum of humanity currently incarnate. Those not incarnate are in no need of the things we intend to say. Those who will never encounter these words will not miss them. So it is only those who are directed towards this material who will materially benefit. And we mean "materially" in its metaphoric, not literal, sense.

We come now to a consideration of those factors which may block and imperil the distribution of this material. Fortunately, the factors are few during the current stage in the history of this small country. Internationally, they are even less. And it was for that purpose these individuals decided to locate themselves far from the centres of the planet, which would otherwise potentially have acted to minimise its distribution.

That said, we may continue in our task for this period, consisting of this coming week and the subsequent week. We anticipate it will be necessary to come again to this Matapaua location, for at this time of year it is suitably quiet. There are no others present nor anticipated. The isolation and seclusion are optimal, the comfort more than sufficient, the sea and wildlife conducive to these explorations in time and space.

That is all for this day.

After a two hour sit, and an hour's sleep, I'm ready for food. It's sunny outside now, after morning rain showers. The wind has turned westerly following the last two days of the warm northerly.

I have just done my first circuit through the glades. Saw three sheep and no houses, plus pig rootings, one keruru, and the usual shags in their colony.

The road has been upgraded in crucial locations, but I saw no sign of property sales. I am unfit and must walk more over these hills while I can.

29 April

I have started rereading The Tao of Physics by Fritjof Capra. It is cold this morning at 14^C. That will make it hard to distinguish the chill signal, except that is felt internally as well as superficially. And yet that is what I was feeling, as indicated by the following transcript:

Rereading Capra is an essential first step for entering an analytical mindset and re-igniting your curiosity regarding the deep domains of description concerning both agapéic space and the realm of reality associated with the questions that you have come here to have answered.

The domain of these questions is extensive. Answering them requires that a boundary-free condition be established within your mind. That is not yet available, so we have set you the task of attending to the explanatory language offered in that text [The Tao of Physics] by which to take your awareness away from the mundane, away from the local, away from the body's senses and preferences, and towards extremity in all parameters. This may be achieved by expanding your awareness away from the familiar towards the foreign and even the nonsensical. We use that last term in the special sense of being unrelated to the senses.

The mind is, in fact, free to soar into any realm at any moment, for any duration, within any time frame. This means that all of existence is accessible to the unconstrained mind. The frameworks of thought generated by locality, by embodiment, by emotion, by relationship – all these act to constrain the mind and its reach.

That provides sufficient reason for the common need to self-isolate in order to bring those unconstrained realms into view. That also gives rise to the need here to have mind-expanding literature at hand, in order to refocus, as you did earlier on the night sky, because your perception is then not confined to within the atmosphere. And it serves to remind, as it did this identity earlier this morning, that there are realms upon realms of distance, of phenomena, of locations far away, of unimaginable magnitude accessible to the senses, only waiting the tools by which to bring them close and make them observable. Those tools (for example, a telescope) are not available to this individual. But the exercise was sufficient to re-mind him of the extent to which the world is bigger than this room, this body, these emotions, and these thoughts. The universe is correspondingly larger. The realm of all that is is unimaginably larger again. So, through this reminder, we bring that entire realm back into the central awareness as the vista to be explored during our time here.

Accordingly, become settled into that magnitude of awareness. And cease the now established self-confinement into the limits of the present sensory systems of the body and the local awareness of the mind. For this is the challenge, to exceed those known things. That is all.

I sat in meditation for some time, then after a chill signal had the following model arrive to my awareness. I have always had difficulty with the idea of the interpenetration of the physical by the spiritual. This model appears to address that by providing a tangible metaphor.

This is in relation to the question of interpenetration. A model for the inter-penetration of spiritual reality with the physical domain is that the physical domain may be envisaged as particles of water in the form of fog or cloud, distributed through air which provides the underlying medium. Spiritual reality constitutes the air, being a continuous medium of finer material in relation to the particulate nature of physical reality, which could perhaps be thought of as comprising atoms represented by the particles of water within fog or cloud.

This provides a tangible and recognisable model. Most people have ex-perienced being in fog or cloud. So they have direct knowledge of the fine particulate nature of fog particles, of the magnitudes involved, and of the finer nature of air within which fog particles are suspended.

And so the idea of the universal field, if one could construe it as that, is of air interpenetrating the mass of fog or cloud. This is a useful model to explain the way in which physical reality is distributed through the under-lying spiritual reality. Variations in the density of the fog may be thought of as representing variations in density within the physical domain, which is supported by, and distributed through, the underlying spiritual reality.

I have sat, slept more, and walked on the beach. Reactions against this discipline are starting to surface. How to occupy the time? I guess read more of the text.

20:28. Have eaten, then slept. I woke from unlikely dreams, then meditated for a while. I asked for cleansing and alignment with my purpose for being here. I feel I'm making little progress in attaining a state required for the effective channelling of deep questions, but will persist. I know that at any time I will be accessed and that it is not my will that counts in this process. And then I immediately felt chilled and received the following:

> We come to give reassurance that the process is proceeding adequately, if not well. Establishing this as a purposeful activity has generated a state of resistance and unwillingness in the individual. These barriers and hurdles need to be overcome before the bulk of the material will be transferred. We anticipate one day more is all that is required. The sleeping is a form of resistance. We suggest it be dispensed with.

So that is plain.

23:41. I've just finished an extended meditation in which I wound up saying, "I give up. Do with me as you will." Later that seemed to enable an opening out of awareness into haric space, freeing the sense of connection to this physical place, feeling a sense of movement, the capacity to move and go where I chose.

So I chose to visit Y. I saw her lying sleeping and simultaneously in her spirit-self manifesting alert joyful awareness, sitting up as in a cherubic self, co-occupying some of her body space as if she were sitting on the same bed surface she was lying on. Felt very loving towards her and saw her change to a delicate shade of pink on the receipt or perception of that affection. It was lovely.

Then elected to visit Keith, and whereas Y. was far on my right side, Keith seemed a little left and he was on the same level, whereas Y was a little lower. It seemed appropriate to soothe Keith, as I think he felt a little frightened of his perception of a foreign presence on the spiritual level.

I'll sleep now. It's been a very good meditation.

30 April
I have just finished transcribing last night's meditation. Chilled now.

> We have some comments we could make if you chose?

Yes, please.

With the completion of that transcript we would now move on to other matters. We have before us a large task. We therefore suggest that this morning be devoted to beginning the complex task of attending to Keith Hill's questions. We propose that the material be brought out and pre-viewed by reading through it so as to refresh yourself, and us through your eyes, of the explicit detail of every part of that material. When that is done we will have more to say.

CHAPTER TWO

On the Physical Universe

Q 1. Currently, observations of the universe have led scientists to propose that the physical universe was created by a Big Bang, in which all matter in the universe came into existence via a singularity. Do you agree with this proposition?

There are many possible ways in which the physical universe may be regarded. One is via a steady-state model with oscillations. Another is to take a fragment of that time frame and consider the model for one cycle of expansion followed by contraction. A third is to take an overall field view of the multitude of universes which independently, without interaction, proceed through cycles of expansion, followed by collapse.

We suggest that a field view is the most comprehensive available. From that perspective, and within an appropriate time frame, it is possible to view the expansions and contractions occurring in an uncoordinated, even chaotic or noisy manner, each contributing to an ongoing exploration of the range designed to be explored, that range consisting of the mechanical, physically optimal arrangements by which to provide environments for myriad life forms. [SEE FIGURE 2.1]

From this perspective there is no attachment to the outcome of any single life form. These are experiments, if you will, conducted from a level in which there is curiosity and goodwill. But there is complete disregard for the birth and death of species, let alone individuals, each being seen as a set of opportunities for constructing ever more varied life forms and providing the means to accumulate the information thus generated.

On a timescale that includes the manifold expansion and contraction phases of multiple universes, arrayed for an observer as if on the edge of a field, the time scales are beyond human comprehension, with no numbers

PETER'S VISION OF THE MULTIVERSE

In this sketch, the uniform background is the featureless unmanifest and the spheres are the manifest multiple universes asynchronously and repeatedly expanding and contracting at their individual rate. That rate was approximately 1 to 3 seconds. Each universe manifested a similar maximum diameter before collapsing again. The web represents the tethering process of sustained intention to the *observer* in this experiment in the field of existence.

The implication is that in the same way that one would locate significant numbers of firecrackers somewhat distant from a house for simple reasons of safety, so also in that field of observation the undetermined behaviour of the universes would be placed at some distance from the *observer* for safety in the experimental setup.

Space seemed unlimited above, below and all around, being everywhere uniform in character. The *observer* was not observed by me but was known to be there. The individual universes seemed somehow tethered to the edge of the viewing field, equidistant in a radial arc from the locus of perception by the *observer*. I sensed my view was partial, but have no way of knowing what lay beyond the limits of my perception, although there were no other features visible in that scene.

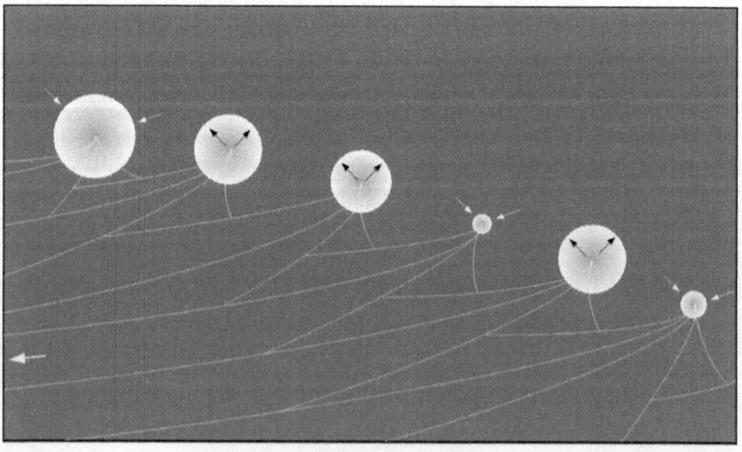

FIGURE 2.1

being applicable. Suffice to describe it thus. Suffice to see it as a large scale experiment. Suffice that there is benign goodwill at the outcome, which is not predetermined.

This being the case, the development of physical life is a probable and unsupported phenomenon. To that extent, the entire field of expectations generated by the human has no meaning other than to the human – and for the purpose of that statement we define "the human" as the species in its long term development and decline. In just the same way as for the human, innumerable other species experience the phenomenon of the emergence of awareness (sentient awareness, we should clarify), its progressive development into alert intelligence, and then its demise within the life cycle of their associated star.

The gathering of information is left not to individuals in the sense that humans understand themselves to be an individual, but to individuality at the group soul level, for that is what survives. The group soul becomes the repository of the accumulated information which, in its turn, is transferred to the next higher level to which it is responsible. And we may not articulate anything at all about that process, or the phenomenon of transfer, or the destination of the information. Suffice to say that it happens, and that it constitutes the meaning for all of the activity of growth, emergence, decay and demise.

Across all the species that have ever existed and that will ever exist – that they develop sentience and consciousness, that there emerges a spiritual container for their consciousness, and that the information accumulated is then retained at a higher level – to this extremely long-term and broad perspective we would add only this: it is a circular phenomenon.

Within the perspective accessible by the human, it is the expansionary impulse that provides the natural underlying motive for the emergence, development and conclusion of every species.

Q 2. Current cosmology suggests that the universe is expanding and that there are three potential outcomes for this expansion: (a) the universe will expand indefinitely, eventually dissipating in what is termed "heat death"; (b) the universe will expand to a certain point, reach equilibrium, and remain "hovering" at this point forever; (c) the universe will expand to a maximum point then start contracting, eventually being re-absorbed into a singularity, an event termed the "big crunch". In a variation of this last option, Stephen Hawkings argues (d) that the universe will contract to a point short of the singularity, then spontaneously expand again, in an event termed the "big bounce". What are your thoughts on these options?

We consider we have addressed options (a) to (d) in the foregoing response to Q 1. However, there are additional points which we will pursue.

The first is that there is no such thing as heat death. What is referred to by that statement is merely the return to the singularity.

The second point is that where the number of expansion and contraction cycles reaches a very large number, then the utility of the experiment has expired because, within that range of conditions for which that universe was designed to explore, sufficient data has been captured. Therefore the expansion is not re-initiated. This is not to imply that an expansion requires initiation. It may be equally valid to state that the contraction is truncated. Nevertheless, and on the time scales referred to, these distinctions are of purely academic interest, having no real validity.

Q 3. Currently, scientists can only observe around 3% of the total matter that they calculate is present in the universe. The missing 97% is termed dark matter and dark energy. What is your view of what we human beings are currently missing from our scientific observations of the physical universe?

Dark matter can be considered to be that energy which is not manifest in physical form. But just because it is not in a manifest physical form does not mean that it has no influence on the functioning of the universe's gravitational forces.

There is no theoretical reason for the dark matter ever to be manifest, precisely because it is unmanifest, and deliberately so. It is not necessary for dark matter to come into manifestation because what is evident is sufficient. It can be considered a mass reservoir by which appropriate conditions may be generated for the development of that particular universe.

The fixed ratio of dark matter to observable matter is one which is purely convenient in order to specify the conditions which are explored in that particular universe. In another universe the ratio would be determined differently, with a corresponding variation in the conditions achieved in that universe. And, naturally, it is not feasible to say anything meaningful about the distinctions between one universe and another, for the main focus of this discussion is the current universe of which you are a part and not any other. Even though other universes are referred to, they will not be discussed.

There are several fundamental parameters of the physical universe. First is existence. Existence may be defined as energy. Energy manifests in either electromagnetic or electrophysical forms. The electromagnetic spectrum is well-known and requires no further explanation here.

The electrophysical constitutes the solidified particles which pop into existence, as has been assumed in the concept of the zero-point field. Those physical particles have a lifetime, which in most instances is very short – we speak in the order of 10^{-9} of a second. This period is perceived as a continuity when the particles' manifestation is averaged into a time period that corresponds to the minimum perceptual bandwidth of the human sensing system. That averaging function is what permits human beings, and individuals of other physical species, to observe matter as solid and continuous.

But the fact remains that individual particles' ephemeral existence, averaged over time, is not evident to ordinary human perception. The magnitude of duration of the existence of any individual particle may be perceived, if we may use that term, anthropomorphic though it is, only by advanced instrumentation, the sensitivity of which has a greater sampling duration than the existence of the particle.

The resolution of sensitivity is the issue here. Automated or instrumented sensory apparatuses that extend human perception reliably deliver evidence of a particle's existence only when the duration of the sampling period is much shorter than the duration of the observed particle. When the sampling period is of the order of a thousand times less than the duration of the observed particle, the resulting data may confidently be used to identify the existence of an individual particle.

Given that this data is readily available to today's technologies, a set of metaphors may be detailed that updates what was imparted in ancient times. In offering these metaphors we continue our task of updating the Bhagavad Gita and other related writings that have accumulated over the last five thousand years, particularly early within that time frame.

In those days perceptions were given to individual minds poorly equipped to register all the relevant connected concepts. Nonetheless, multiple recipients of those perceptions agreed sufficiently to generate the descriptions that have endured to the present. But given that due to the exponential rise in technologies, to the numbers of participants utilising those technologies, and to the research budgets which support continued measuring, information on record today is a thousand million times what has been accumulated throughout human history. So there is now a vastly larger data-set of perceptions from which to extrapolate relevant concepts.

Therefore we say, in support of the present accumulated data, that there is no need to share further speculations. Concepts are already in circulation that satisfactorily interpret existing measurements. These measurements provide confidence that ephemeral particles do in fact exist – with the caveat already expressed in terms of the adequacy of sampling.

Accordingly, from our perspective, it is enough to state that there are an extraordinarily large number of particles, which are more or less uniformly distributed throughout the known and the unknown universe, and that the evidence for this statement is contained within the perceived phenomena of stars, galaxies, and similar features of the observed and known universe.

Of course, this assertion also extends beyond what can be observed, because the manifest universe is larger than will ever be perceived by human beings. Nevertheless, in terms of a limiting parameter for establishing a theoretical understanding of the field of existence, we suggest the ratio of the known universe to the unknown universe is of the order of one to a thousand. So the universe is not infinite, and there is no reason to imagine it to be so. The fact that it is not infinite is predicated on the fact that the universe's time-field is generated from the singularity referred to earlier.

However, the universe's expansion is on such a time scale that the existence of the human species is rendered almost invisible when its location on the universe's expanding time line is considered. Accordingly, human understanding of the extent of the universe's time field is necessarily limited.

Nevertheless, the time field exists, the ephemeral particle field exists, the distinction between visible and invisible particles primarily involves perceiving energy manifested in particle field events, and the determination of the universe's particle field across its population of individual particle spectra (using "spectra" to indicate the range of particle energies associated with the ephemeral particle field) is a question of the sensitivity of the measuring systems currently employed. At present these systems render the bulk of the manifest particles invisible. Only perceived particles are identified as manifest. The unperceived particles are currently identified as dark matter. As detection methodologies increase in sensitivity a greater proportion of currently unobserved ephemeral particle events will be discovered.

Therefore the three percent figure will progressively increase, although not to a final one hundred percent. As a result, the notion that there exists a range of manifest energy will grow in the thinking of theoreticians. We note that duration is not the key to identifying currently undetected particles, but that the energy manifested by individual particles is the issue. All are similarly ephemeral. But the energy contained within each varies.

This constitutes the answer to the question about dark matter and its existence. To use the metaphor of the watery sea, the universe is a veritable sea of significance of which only the universe's highest wave-tips are detected. The rest is not.

Q 4. How old is the universe? Cosmologists project that the Big Bang occurred around 14 billion years ago. On the other hand, the universe may have previously "bounced" a number of times, making it older than 14 billion years. Your thoughts?

Given that it has no meaning to specify how many expansion and contraction cycles the current universe has proceeded through, there is no point in attempting to signify the age of the universe apart from within the current expansionary phase. In that sense, the expansionary phase has been occurring for about 40 billion years. The exact number is not of particular relevance. The errors in the scientific estimates to date are due to measurements not yet made.

The death of the human species will occur within the lifetime of this particular star, which will occur long before this universe experiences the peak of its expansionary phase. Therefore the time frame which has meaning for humanity is that of its arising and its destruction by that local star. There is no possibility of escape from that event. It is sufficiently distant to concern no one, even to the five hundredth generation from now. Therefore, again, it has no true meaning.

Q 5. Cosmologists emphasise that the physical universe is expanding. Yet there is also an attractive force, which on the physical level we term gravity and which we understand to be a force that is somehow a property of matter, or somehow connected to it. While we don't actually know what gravity is, we ascribe to gravity the power to draw cosmic dust into suns, and suns into galaxies, and galaxies into super-galaxies. We consider gravity also formed the Earth and Moon into spherical shapes, and keeps the Earth circling the Sun, etc. Newton described gravity as a mysterious force that acts at a distance, while Einstein described gravity as a curvature in space-time. These are descriptions of its manifestations rather than a definition of what it is in and of itself. What is your definition of gravity?

The experimental conditions for this multiverse are such as to confine a maximum expansion within certain limits. Those limits have been determined within the context of each universe in question. There is a relationship between the expansionary impulse, which is the fundamental reason for the singularity to expand, and gravity, which is there to organise the resultant structure, whatever that structure may be. And so gravity acts both locally and at astronomical distances. The attraction experienced by one component of matter for another component of matter is a variation on the attraction of matter for itself. Given that the original bulk of the mass was located at a centroid, then the far-flung extremities still in their trajectory are nevertheless experiencing that self-constraining force. And in due course that force will be responsible for the recollection back into a contractionary phase.

The nature of the attractive force is no different from what has already been determined. The range of the attractive force is without limit. And so when the momentum of the expansionary phase balances the attractive force, that will signal the transition from expansionary phase to contractionary phase.

The issue is partly the dark matter and/or dark energy which remains the focal point at the centre of the universe. Given that that has yet to be identified, although its properties are observable, the apparent local attraction will be seen to be only a small part of the attraction of that central mass. Explicit within this is a lack of understanding of the properties of the universe's remnant central core. Its temperature is within one degree of absolute zero. Its radiance is therefore undetectable. Human investigation of the universe, from this small planet revolving around this small star on a radial arm of a galaxy far from the centre of the universe, has not yet penetrated far enough to begin to observe, let alone measure, conditions towards the centre of the universe as a whole. It is the fact of limited observation that prevents full appreciation of the dynamics at play.

The attractive forces between matter are already known. They do not differ between elements, molecules, atoms, etc, in this region of the universe compared to any other region of the universe. The factor which brings coherence to the universe's entire dynamic of expansion and contraction is simply unobserved to date.

Regarding a definition of gravity, our definition is that ultimately gravity is a repulsive force inverted. Its nature derives from the population of ephemeral particles which are in themselves repulsive to one another. There is a balance point between the sea of ephemeral particles, which may also be termed a mesh. This mesh consists of the multidimensional arising and decay of ephemeral particles. There are also mass effects and tides within this mesh that cannot be quantified. Nevertheless, these local

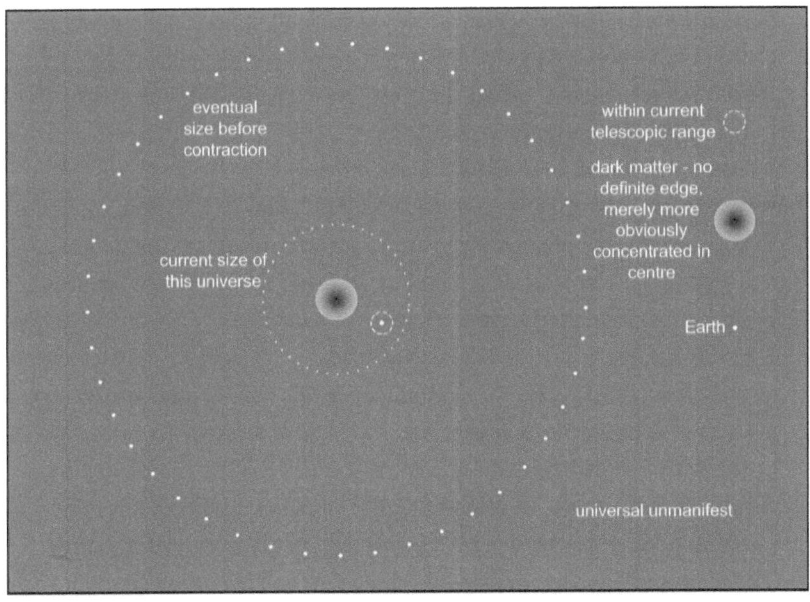

FIGURE 2.2

expanding and contracting fields render non-uniform the otherwise uniform mesh of individual particle events.

What is being referred to here are large field effects, which may be thought of as tidal effects within the ebb and flow of space-time. The mesh of ephemera is continuously uniform. But the mass effects are subject to dispersed oscillation at various frequencies. On the mass level, those dispersed oscillations lead to localized concentrated forces, the consequence of which generate other local diminished zones. Consequently, what is observed as higher or lower density zones in the otherwise uniform field of manifest ephemeral particles constitutes what are observed as physical concentrations within space-time.

Concentrated zones represent radiated, and therefore observable, locations distributed across the physical universe, which are identified as suns, planets and galaxies. The diminished zones are the space between such solar and extra-solar phenomena. Accordingly, these phenomena, which provide relative physical solidity in the universe, are a product of differential density states in the background particle ephemera.

At the level of large-scale population dynamics, these tidal effects of the ephemeral particles are subject to very long-term periodicity, compared to which an Earth century is as a nanosecond, or less. So these events occupy time scales that are of theoretical significance only. Nevertheless, the question assigns meaning to these events. The meaning sought is found in the observed manifest universe.

The existence of concentrated nodes, if they may be referred to as such, within the matrix of ephemeral particle population distribution, creates the opportunity for life of all kinds to come into existence. The numbers and kinds of life increase over the time scales in question, as a result of evolution affecting species development.

To repeat, the sampling period constituted by the human lifetime is so short that it is impossible for any embodied individual to observe, in any practical way, the nature and rate of change in oscillation of energy existing in the manifest universe. These matters can be addressed only on the theoretical level, as we are attempting to do now. It is a task many minds have struggled with, inhibited as they necessarily have been by their narrow sensing systems and by the extremely brief duration of their existence.

From the broader perspective that we have adopted and choose to comment from, there exists an endless process of manifestation into physical existence, which results in changes in the fields of existing energy. These changes may be observed by the human (or by any other species) as data brought to its modes of awareness or, in its processed form, as information brought to the aware mind. Were a sufficiently long-term view able to be established by any individual body-mind, the oscillations in location and the density of ephemeral particles would be observable on a ten thousand million year time frame of change. From that timescale, in a manner similar to time-lapse photography, one could capture the changes occurring in a sequence of observations, which could then be visually interpreted as the flux and flow, expansion and return, of a turbulent sea. This is the nature of the change. The difficulty is the limited duration of the perceptions generated by an observing biologically-based mind.

Therefore, the notion of gravity is valid on the local scale. It is somewhat less valid on the interstellar or intergalactic scale, as on that scale the more random nature of the deep oscillations, if one may apply that term, leads to a natural fluctuation in regional density of the manifest universe. On the broader scale, then, deep oscillations function as a hidden influence that underlies local and regional gravitational effects. By this we postulate a less accessible field of influence in the manifestation of the universe into visibility.

Q 6. What is your definition of space? Does space expand to enable matter in the form of galaxies to travel further away from each other? Or is more space "manufactured" to provide the space for the universe to expand?

Our definition of space is a field of existence within which activity can occur. From the perspective of the image projected into this mind [SEE FIGURE 2.1] whereby the multiple universes are arrayed in space going about their progressive expansion and collapse, we see no need to postulate that there is any shortage of space, which is the implicit and underlying attitude relating to any question regarding whether space must be manufactured. There is no shortage of space!

Q 7. What is the function of black holes? What happens to the energy at their heart? And are there white holes that, opposite to black holes, emanate energy?

We have no intention of responding to the myth of the black hole and the varieties of speculation that have arisen in attempting to understand their function and purpose. We regard the phenomenon as entirely natural. It is a long-term phenomenon. When it accumulates enough matter it changes state. And that is the extent of our description. We postulate no existence of white holes.

Q 8. Scientists assume that the universe is a closed system. What is your view?

We regard the universe to be a closed system. It is complete within itself. It requires nothing obtainable externally. The developmental internal forces are entirely adequate to drive all behaviour.

CHAPTER THREE

Interlude: One

1 May

It is cold this morning. There's a southerly wind, and it is clear. Yesterday I found a yellowhammer sitting on the grass by the house next door. I stepped quietly past it and wondered if it was dying, although its eyes were open and observing me. This morning I realised it had probably been stunned by flying into the glass balustrade around the deck. When I checked I was pleased to see it had gone.

My resistance is strong this morning. I arose, had a big plate full of oats and juice, lay down in spite of the inner voice instructing me not to, and slept for another hour and a half!

I have found a baby-changing mattress to rest my knees on when I sit. That felt comfortable, but the cold, along with the white-faced herons hunting insects on the mingi-mingi, were distracting.

I have started playing with flour. With no eggs or butter, for dinner I mixed wholemeal flour with sugar, oil and water and pan toasted them into little rocks, then mixed them with tuna. Filling, nutritious and chewy. But not delicious.

Having found *Islam, A Short History* by Karen Armstrong on the bookshelf, I read some of it. Photographed drawings made so far. Will enhance them via computer in due course.

20:03. Have sat in meditation for some time and felt happy after asking for a blessing on this place to last five hundred years. I saw and specified a zone of harmony extending with spherical radius of this house to the road hilltop. And decided to gift a copy of *Agapé and the Hierarchy of Love* to the house library in appreciation of my time here. Over the years, staying in such optimal conditions has been so productive for me. After I put down the dictaphone I immediately felt chilled and was advised to rest.

2 May

This morning I felt I needed to read more of The Tao of Physics before continuing with the questions. I am starting the section on space-time, which is appropriate given the content of Question 9.

I feel there is more to extract from the air-fog model than I have thought of so far, particularly in relation to dynamics within it. So I sat in meditation for a while, visualising relativities in movement, the creation of local frames of reference, etc, projecting it to astronomical scales. I felt confused, but received an intimation that clarity will be provided later.

> In interpreting the multiverse image, convey the connection between the central *observer* and the array of cycling universes as a mesh through which the entire individual universe can be observed. The mesh forms no barrier to observation. A thin tracery of white or pale grey lines would be appropriate for the mesh, only slightly visible against the essentially dark background. Regarding the air-fog image, more detail will be given later.

For a number of days I've felt significant turbulence in the dantian. It feels a bit as though that is being stepped up, perhaps in order to enable these responses.

I've imaged taking flight into the space around the Earth, but remaining attached to it as if a satellite on a string, whirling around far out into space, then riding the satellite flung in a circle around the lower portion of the Earth, then accelerating ahead of it, then dropping behind, feeling a state of playfulness, just to explore what was possible.

Next I cast my point of attention far beyond that again, so I could observe the process of being flung around. I then slowed down my internal perceptual rate, which extended my sampling period so much that the rotations of the swung satellite body on its string appeared as a solid disc due to going so rapidly around. As an exercise in changing the rate of perception, or the thought rate to alter experience of time, it was a successful manipulation of imaginal space.

3 May

Last night I read Capra where he quotes Krishna in the Bhagavad Gita: "But I am not bound by this vast work of creation. I am and I watch the drama of works." I feel that identifiably describes what I was shown of the multiverse experiment.

I texted Keith to advise progress. Washed clothes. It is cold and clear this morning, with a southerly wind. My fingers are stiff, so I'm typing slowly. It is 11ᶜ inside. Modified the multiverse drawing according to instructions from yesterday. Turned on the heater after cleaning the plug contacts to prevent fire.

10:58. As soon as I sat down for a second half hour of meditation this morning, I pulled my woolly hat right down over my eyes and, with my eyes shut, into my awareness sprang a field of bright blue interlaced with a fine pattern of gold threads. I think I've not seen that before. It's certainly not what I see when I open my eyes now. I presume it's a perception through the ajna. My question is, what is this for? And in the back of my mind I know that this is a simple perceptual tool. The bright blue has gone now. It was very distinctive to begin with, a lovely bright eggshell blue, one might call it. So the question is, what is that perceptual tool best and most appropriately used for?

We would respond to that. These perceptions and perceptual tools are given to you for your own illumination and awareness. They are utilised on this occasion specifically for you to come to know things which have been known at other times through these identical processes. It is a method of coming to know through repetition. This protocol of repetitive awareness enables the populace at large, should they wish to become informed of these events, techniques, actions and results, to modify their understanding of the nature of the world, along with its underlying constituents and manifest forms. It also enables them to modify their understanding of their place in the world, and to adjust their own behaviour and beliefs into optimal rather than falsified form.

We again come this day into your awareness in order to remind you of these things, to occasionally show you things to sustain your enthusiasm. And we note that you require this, as in these latter days of your life your focus falls short of the intense curiosity required in order to seek beyond the mundane and the superficial to underlying forms, factors and knowledge.

We would that you understand these things and take them deeply into your own being, so as to sustain as best you may the opportunity which still challenges you, to be a beacon of light and hope and understanding through the things that we say through you. For that is the promise and the opportunity: to say again those things said before, but in this language and at this time. For the things themselves do not change. Merely their visibility varies.

We wish to take your attention now to another level in order to acquaint you with activities there.

I then experienced an image of myself as a black wavy-haired handsome white male, as if in a white uniform, self-consciously gorgeous, attracting the attention of women. A poncey character, I thought. Self-affected, full of himself, making the most of the opportunities. I perceived the invitation to come out again, as if to explore the larger self and its qualities. I then experienced a spontaneous inner aspect of myself, enthusiastic, bright-eyed, curious as hell, simply dashing for the barrier, whatever it was, and bursting out into some external vista, flying perhaps as if a bird on wing, gazing with delight on what lay outside. Eager to go far and explore and encounter everything.

We bring these short adventures to a close, simply as a means to illustrate active sub-personalities with desirable characteristics which can be drawn on as necessary or desired. The fearless explorer is the most appropriate and valid aspect by which to engage the attention and stimulate willingness to go beyond the mundane, the known and the superficial, as we have remarked before. This day presents another opportunity to address the questions of the man Keith Hill. We would begin that task now.

CHAPTER FOUR

On Spiritual Reality and the Universe

Q 9. The scientific assumption behind the previous question is that the universe is a closed physical system. Yet there is also the possibility that the cosmos as a whole is a closed system, but that there are layers to the cosmos apart from the physical, that could feed the physical universe. (I am using the word "cosmos" to include everything existing, spiritually and physically.) Your thoughts?

There are many components to that question. We will address them one by one. The aspect we elect to address first is the concept of spiritual reality "feeding" the physical domain or manifest universe. This is true. There would be no physical universe if it were not created and supported in the sense that we have indicated in the initial vision of the multiverse, and if there was no intention by which it was created.

That being the situation, we may amplify it by adding that hidden beneath perception in the multiverse vision is an entire detailed structure which is rather too complex to explain in any depth. Suffice to say that there are nodes – and we will use the language contained within the questions otherwise we depart from any potential for being understood – within the spiritual realm. And we identify for the first time that is the essential nature of that vision. This is its explicit content, that there is a contrast between that and the universes, which are a deliberate creation.

And we regret the reluctance that this particular individual has towards the language of creation versus chance or randomness.

We intend that the meaning associated with the term "creation" is in the experimental sense, not the apocryphal sense, not the god-language sense, nor the sense contained within the argument for or against the idea of creation in its religious sense. We are talking about a context within which there is benign interest in learning something. In order to enable that learning to occur, a structure, a tool, or a machine, is first imagined, then fashioned. The capacity of any individual to engage with this perspective, this mindset, this exercise in curiosity, is what we mean to stimulate when we use the terms "creation" and "created."

We explicitly divorce this discussion from the entire history of the created universe in this language as well as all others, for so many dimensions of that term serve at this time only to confuse. So although we must use the term in its secular sense, if we may term it in that way, or its scientific sense, as we could also designate it, within the realm of the language of discussion, that being the English language used in this particular small corner of the world, we nevertheless elect to utilise that term in a simplified form, explicitly disconnecting it from those other concepts and their associated sets of notions that we have just referred to.

That is the sense in which the physical universe is contained and supported within a domain in which there is manifest intention to explore, to run the experiment, to collect the data, and then to allow the experiment either to self-terminate or to deliberately end it.

So in that sense the physical universe is closed in physical terms, but not closed in terms of being embedded within a broader supportive field and realm of existence. Not that there is any significant transfer of anything other than intention into the confined location of that realm, for the experimental procedure has been to seed the environment in physical terms, and then simply watch it proceed through its various cycles, including expansion and contraction, as well as the resulting opportunities that arise within those cycles for the spontaneous formation of life.

We would briefly expand on this procedure, for it is certainly true that as opportune locations form and provide well-suited environmental niches for species to exploit, so they are seeded, in the sense that organisms are created, and then left to their own devices in these myriad environmental niches. In the same way, pre-human species, being humanity's ancient forebears, were spiritually created, seeded if you will, and then left to their own devices. And as, through the process of emergence, they progressively became ready to be occupied by intellect and purpose, that was done.

The extent to which these experiments have been initiated and carried out is beyond the scope of any individual mind to encompass. So at this time what we communicate is extremely limited. What we can affirm is that the process is dispersed, that it occurs over a multitude of time periods, and that it repeatedly interjects into emerging environmental niches.

So there is ample opportunity to play with the construction, extension and deletion of physically existing species, preparing them to be occupied for intellect and purpose as specified within experimental parameters.

Q 10. The human concept of the spiritual realm is that we have a spiritual core, which existed before our birth in a body and continues to exist after our body dies. Your concept of the spiritual realm is that it is vaster than the physical universe, consists of various levels, and is filled with vast numbers of beings. From your perspective, could you define (a) the nature of the spiritual realm, and (b) the nature of spirit?

There are many entirely satisfactory descriptions of those aspects contained within the monologues and dialogues already given. We see no need to expand upon those because they are sufficient.

The only thing we are inclined to contribute at this point is with respect to (b), regarding the nature of spirit. The essence is human. Spirit in other essences is non-human. Spirit in its highest aspect is traditionally associated with God or the gods. We decline to use those terms because of their confusing connotations.

However, it is true that at the highest level there is identity, there is intelligence, there is intention, and there is awareness and willingness to act in constructive ways so as to acquire information and knowledge. The human is a product of that intention. The multitudes of non-human realms are equally a product of that intention.

The necessity for embodied humans to come to know this is zero. The necessity for human and non-human realms to interact is zero.

And yet from their individual domains, and being curious, they sometimes do so. Many of them cannot, for they are insufficiently co-associated to become aware of each other, due to the embodied aspects of other non-human species being confined to very distant planetary systems in this universe, or in entirely distinct other universes.

Accordingly, there is awareness of the existence of other representative forms of intelligent life. But to expect any listing is inappropriate because it is ineffectual. It is sufficient to acknowledge that there are other perfectly valid centres of intellect and purpose, a very few of which have some knowledge of and capacity to co-associate with the range of the human, and vice versa.

Q 11. It seems to me that the three forces – repulsive, attractive and creative – that I identified in relation to the physical universe also act in relation to the spiritual aspect of reality. On this level, the repulsive force is responsible for humanity's sense of spiritual fallenness, of forgetfulness and separation, and for psycho-spiritual feelings such as lostness, loneliness, ignorance, and despair. Attraction manifests as love and nurturing. And creativity manifests as growth and as the desire to obtain knowledge and to understand. Is this a correct assumption?

We would deny that there is a repulsive force acting on the spiritual level. There is no analogue of that set of forces existing in the physical domain that similarly exists in the spiritual domain. The spiritual domain, we take this opportunity to reaffirm, is based on loving attraction and nothing else.

The psycho-spiritual feelings quoted, such as lostness, loneliness, ignorance and despair, do not result from a sense of spiritual fallenness. The sense of spiritual fallenness itself is a consequence of the residual memory of being in another place. As a consequence of forgetfulness, and due to the barely recalled awareness of the contrasting difference between conditions in the domain of spirit and psycho-social conditions within disorganised humanity, individuals make the projection that there is a condition of being fallen.

Another aspect of this is that, in spiritual terms, humanity is located differently from the location in the clear light. This is another factor that generates the perception of living in a lesser place. Finally, there is the universal social hierarchy, which generates awareness of the privileged few living in better conditions than the general mass of humanity. This contributes to the sense that that other place of the clear light must be better than this. In fact, it is not better. It is simply different.

We accept the description concerning "attraction being a manifestation of love and nurturing, and creativity manifesting as growth and the desire to obtain knowledge and to understand."

Q 12. The Michael books give the name the Dao (also Tao) to the ultimate source of all that exists. The word Dao is preferred because it avoids the idea of a personal God that dominates religious thinking. However, even this term has religious associations. Perhaps in this secular age we should use an abstract noun which has no such connotations: "Origin", "Presence" or "Source". Your thoughts on what the "source of everything" should best be called?

Our preference is in relation to the identification of what we have called the *observer* in the multiverse. That term is perfectly adequate. It is distinct from traditional attributions about god-like nature. It is appropriate in these days of understanding. It represents reality using culturally relevant models. And it fits with the creation of knowledge via the construction of experiments.

We have zero desire to foster any sense of difference between such an *observer* and any manifest spiritual identity, embodied or not, each of which is a focus of intellect and purpose and is just as capable of adopting the role of *observer* and creating original things, including experiments by which to acquire knowledge.

Accordingly, we are content that the term of *observer* is sufficiently neutral, as well as being sufficiently resonant with the connotation-sets appropriate to these times, as to require no change. We therefore recommend its use.

Q 13. With respect to the relationship of the physical realm to the spiritual realm, it appears to me that there are three possibilities:

(a) There is the view that only the physical realm exists, and any talk of spirituality is a fantasy, whether that fantasy takes some kind of religious or New Age form of thinking. This is the scientific empirical view.

(b) There is the view that all reality, both physical and spiritual, consists of one stuff, one material, which is somehow differentiated into separate frequencies, and these differentiated frequencies manifest to human beings as the physical and spiritual levels of reality. This is the non-dualist spiritual perspective.

(c) There is the view that actually only the spiritual realm exists, and the physical realm is a projection by spiritual entities, or created and sustained by them, or is an illusion of some kind. This is the idealist monist view.

Your response to these common perspectives?

We would describe (a) as the scientistic view, not the scientific empirical view. We affirm (b), the non-dualist perspective, specifically because the discussion related to the condensation of physicality from its underlying spiritual source energy is the most appropriate to describe the process of coming into appearance.

A distinction needs to be made between the zero-point field and the realm of spirit, if one can express it in such terms. The zero-point field is not identical to the domain of spirit. There are as yet unformulated descriptions which will facilitate a deeper understanding of the distinction between the two.

However, the first distinction is that the zero-point field is a field of electrospiritual properties manifesting points of condensation into electrophysical properties. The distinction that applies can be described utilising the Laplace transform, as has been done by others. It is the closest approximation to the process by which one can achieve the transition from the domain of spirit into the domain of manifest physicality. By utilising the process of condensation there is an implicit link to the air-fog model we have proposed, that of condensed water vapour within air, by which an unmanifest form comes into visible form via the process of condensation.

We assert that this model is a mental-level model. It is not to be understood literally. Nevertheless, the metaphor is sufficient for individuals who understand the physical phenomenon of condensation to gain some understanding of the way that one kind of domain can manifest another kind of domain, even if the two are not intrinsically different. It is a model of the emergence of the physical from the spiritual, not the creation of a separate domain. While the qualities of the two domains differ, they remain linked.

In that sense, we reject (c), the idealist monist view, because there is no illusion in the manifestation of the physical domain out of spiritual reality. However, the idea that the physical realm is a projection, and is created and sustained, is valid. To that extent, the monist perspective may be considered to be non-dualist and to have validity.

Q 14. Humanity perceives reality from a human perspective. It seems to me that this human view is narrow and limited. We are only aware of 3% of the physical universe. And we are only aware of a tiny sliver of spiritual reality – and even the existence of this is denied by some, while many others superimpose religiously-

derived assumptions over it. In effect, when most of us consider the nature of reality, we are viewing our own assumptions more than even the reduced perspective of reality available to us. Arguably, most of us consciously avoid engaging with any sense of reality as it extends beyond our everyday lives. T.S. Eliot commented on this by stating that human beings cannot stand too much reality. Your thoughts on our perception and approach to reality?

A significant percentage of humanity has no interest in exploring the nature of reality because that is not their life plan. They have other things to do and would potentially be disturbed, even overwhelmed, by a perceptual bandwidth which was broader than what the animal form provides. That is the sense in which to understand the statement T.S. Eliot made that "human beings cannot stand too much reality."

However, there is the remainder, or even the majority, of the world population who are entirely capable of perceiving outside the narrowband perceptual systems of the human bodily organism. The extent to which they find such perceptions enlightening or disturbing is primarily determined by the intellectual perspective of the civilisation in which they live. Where their society is open to perceptions of non-ordinary things, and they are able to discuss them without threat or limitation, then there is no sense in which the human being cannot stand too much reality. Rather, a welcoming perspective may be adopted.

Nonetheless, it is often true that the information obtained via non-ordinary perception, that is, through the auric or spiritual channels of communication, constitutes an intellectual puzzle. The challenge then is to integrate that information, because it may offer a fresh perspective, in contrast to traditional descriptions of non-ordinary patterns of perception. And that is the extent to which it may be disturbing.

The avatar, here redefined as the perceptually gifted individual whose life purpose is to investigate these things, to explore the spectrum of information available via non-ordinary perceptual systems, and then to provide contemporary formulations of it, is the category of individual most empowered by the opportunity and challenge presented by the manifestation of such perceptual gifts. And so it is in this case, with this man and his colleague Keith Hill, who each established a pre-life intention to provide a fresh perspective on these categories of input from the non-organism-based perceptual channels. The development of that intention, the collection of information, the expression of it in academic and literary forms, and the sharing of it through social groups and methods of dissemination, is what they are here for. To the extent that has begun, and has run part way through its intended course, serves merely as an indication of what is possible. Not of what is better. And this is an important distinction.

Every person has their own intention. Every person has their own life plan to investigate and bring to fruition, so as to achieve their objectives and live a satisfying life. It is not the case to any degree at all that one is better than another! The only distinction to be made is the degree to which an individual may, through whatever means, know that their life has a purpose, that they have a particular and personal set of intentions related to their life, and feel that they are appropriately occupied in those activities so as to achieve a satisfactory outcome for their life.

One life plan is not necessarily the same as any other's. Reality is so complex in all its dimensions that there are myriad opportunities, and one person can never investigate them all. Therefore there is quite sufficient room for all individuals to occupy themselves with their life plan, and to derive understanding and satisfaction from that, and to achieve a sense of completion at the end of their life, if they are able to do so.

The contemporary social world is doing humanity a disservice to the extent that it mitigates or denies the spiritual purpose of humanity. Within this context it is appropriate to identify that fact, because every embodied individual is spirit first, foremost and always. Accordingly, all individuals have a life plan as part of their spiritual purpose, via which they manifest their intention. And to the extent that the modern education system neglects to inform participants that this is the case, they do every individual so affected a disservice.

We would hold this out as a preferred protocol by which every individual can receive official empowerment, if we may express it in that way, to identify their purpose and thereby feel empowered, and righteously so, to investigate these aspects of their life, and to continue to do so. This is distinct from the social objectives of procreation, we would hasten to add. Although those two things are often linked, they are not invariably so.

CHAPTER FIVE

Interlude: Two

3 May

20:32. I have had a long sit this evening in which I sought to eliminate all exaggeration in my appetites. I also sought to cleanse my organism and attributes with the energy of the eggshell-blue (aqua?) and gold. That colour combination is intrinsically and unashamedly spiritual. I'll find a way to incorporate it into the AgapéSchoolinz website.

Interestingly, the term "unashamedly" came spontaneously in relation to the aqua/gold combination. It reveals the extent to which I have been ashamed of, or tried to hide, and definitely avoid, flaunting my spiritual aspirations and beliefs. But I also presume it is a reaction to having lifetimes shortened at other times. So it may possibly be a simple consequence of old fear now misplaced.

4 May

04:26. For reasons which have been unclear to me I have been quite wakeful this night. I've just woken from a dream in which the scene was of a dance or theatre club where there had been a clandestine takeover by people without obvious financial means of doing so, given the level of finance involved in paying off the prior performers, consisting of a $20,000 payment. The takeover had clearly been orchestrated so as to provide a pre-rehearsed show by strangers. I was incensed, but by that point I had been effectively relegated to the margins, being disenfranchised and powerless to do anything other than watch as an entirely new style was inaugurated – a new song and dance routine.

I woke out of that dream and was reminded of Karen Armstrong's book on Islam and its development, which describes endless political processes and battles of various kinds during the establishment phase of that religion.

I'm aware that the material that has arrived in my awareness constitutes a potentially exploitable and marketable opportunity for anybody who could see the potential in it, and that it could be bent to those purposes in the same way as every single religion through time has been. And if there is money in it then people after money will come. So I am reminded that what is being brought out of the 'ether' here, although I feel it to be significant and would like to share it, probably means that someone else would like to take it from me if they can. Beliefs are a touchy territory, and even though there has been explicit mention in recent days of the lack of threat, or at least the availability of freedom to share this material, that doesn't mean that other people won't have completely contrary ideas.

06:09. I just thought of the emphasising of the role of querent on the website. A definition of querent could be: A participant in prospecting for experiential learning; one who takes part in the group with the explicit expectation that through group activities they may gain information useful to their life; one who is present with an attitude of openness to learning from within themselves and from the other participants around them.

07:28. Completed the above transcripts. What an interesting time I'm having!

10:34. I have oiled the front door hinges. I then cleaned and oiled and reset the kitchen sliding door track and rollers so it moves freely. Waxed the sticky kitchen drawers, washed my jeans, and walked on the beach. Will now will sit for the next episode.

10:45. As soon as I shut my eyes I became aware of seeing the swirling currents of what seemed to be a suspension of sand in water, orangey-brown particles in ceaseless motion within the eddies and flow of what appears to be a gently turbulent current, interestingly predominantly moving from left to right. There appears to be a textured background behind it, as if looking through water to a stream bed containing stones or similar. The question is, what lies behind that? And what is this material – the liquid, the suspended particles? I seem to be stationary in relation to the background texture. I wonder if this is the stream of dhamma, a tributary to the river. Who knows? *[Note: Dhamma, also spelt dharma, has various meanings, including referring to the nature of all reality, to the laws that govern nature and reality, and to practices by which knowledge and experience of what underpins all reality is gained.]*

We come to amplify this observation. This vision is of a mere backwater in the metaphor of dhamma. You have been in that river and into that sea many years ago, during a Vipassana retreat. This vision represents the consequence of protectionism inherent in the musings of this morning. Such protectionism has always delimited opportunities for the expression of dhamma – descriptions of spiritual reality and its relation to humanity, to use an English phrase – and confined its influence to a mere backwater.

What we are offering is international scope. The only important thing is uploading the material to the website for anyone to interpret it how they may. These matters need to be settled in this mind before there can be a proper return to the questions in process. That is all.

5 May

08:03. I slept twelve hours last night, so I'm feeling quite peaceful this morning. I woke from long dreams involving my former workplace and the stresses and frustrations there, but also the personnel and my good relations with them. One was being given new clothes. I felt I should check the obituary pages on my return.

I've wiped the windows, but they look no better. Then cleaned the lounge windows properly, which is much better. I can see clearly now. Today is to be a quiet day. Time to transcribe.

10:04. I've just realised that an interpretation of the statement that "the *observer* has no concern for species, let alone individuals" is that that is not its function. Which would accommodate the statements garnered from the subjects in Michael Newton's books [i.e. *Journey of Souls* and *Destiny of Souls*]regarding those, perhaps, higher selves or entities beyond, who were responsible for the design of species, for example fish. "I'm quite good with fish."

We would interrupt these speculations, accurate though they are, by continuing with the questions.

CHAPTER SIX

A Proposed Model
of Reality

[Note: The model presented in this chapter was conceived before the previous answers were given. So it doesn't incorporate their content. However those answers have introduced ideas in preparation for a response to the following questions.]

My view is that we need a new model of reality that incorporates both the empirical discoveries of the sciences and the nature of spirituality, using terminology that makes sense in today's world. This model needs to accommodate the concepts of quantum vacuum, emergence and evolution, and also connect the physical and spiritual, to present a comprehensive description of multidimensional reality.

The model I offer here [See FIGURE 6.1] is my attempt to think through what such a model might look like. It is a sketch. My approach is derived from Neoplatonic emanationist thinking, in which everything that exists is derived from the One or Pure Being. The concept of eight levels of emanations draws on the idea of octaves taught by G.I. Gurdjieff.

Level 1 is the atomic and sub-atomic levels of the physical world.

Level 2 consists of the tendencies innate in the cosmos, such as creativity that has generated marvellous diversity throughout the universe. Creativity gives rise to evolution, complexity and emergence.

Level 3 is the third dimension of physical existence. The fascinating aspect of this is that due to the cosmos' innate creativity, not only is there an astonishing diversity of forms and creatures, but there are also orders of organisation. So on Earth we have minerals, amoeba, slimes, vegetation, insects, reptiles, mammals, and human beings, each of which exist on increasingly complex levels of material and biological organisation. The result is teeming life.

Level 4 is the realm of thought. This is the level at which we human beings make sense of our experiences of reality.

Level 5 is the spiritual realm. I make two assumptions about this level. First, like level three, it is teeming with spiritual life, in whatever forms they may exist. Second, just as there are orders of organisation within the third dimension, the higher orders of which are incomprehensible to lower orders (i.e. bacteria can have no conception of the existence of ants, and ants can have no conception of human existence), so it appears reasonable to assume that there are orders of organisation on this level in which lower orders of spiritual being would have no idea of the existence and experience of higher orders of being.

It is clear patterns are present within each of the levels of the manifest cosmos, patterns that govern what happens within each level and that define the boundaries of

8th level magnitude	ABSOLUTE TRANSCENDENT CONSCIOUSNESS Tao / Pure Being	Origin of all that is
7th level magnitude	ACTIVE CONSCIOUSNESS Active Tao / Active Being	Manifests the cosmos
6th level magnitude	Forces - principles - laws	Organising principles
5th level magnitude	Spiritual realm	Spiritual entities
	THE MANIFEST COSMOS	
4th level magnitude	Thought - Space-time	Medium of thought
3rd level magnitude	Matter - volume - bodies	Physical existence
2nd level magnitude	Inherent propensities	Creativity, emergence
1st level magnitude	Constituent matter and energy of universe	Atomic, sub-atomic, quantum vacuum

FIGURE 6.1

what is possible in each. These patterns are discernable mathematically, biologically, cosmically, sub-atomically, socially, conceptually, artistically, and so on. Their existence suggests that a higher level of organisation underpins the manifest cosmos. This higher order of organisation I have identified as the 6th and 7th levels.

The 6th level consists of the principles that underpin the manifest cosmos. Scientist Martin Rees had suggested that just six numbers underpin the physical universe. My model proposes that these numbers were projected from the 6th level.

The 7th level I postulate as the active force, or power, or consciousness, or whatever we wish to call whatever manifested the cosmos.

The 8th level is Dao, the mysterious "whatever it is" that underpins all of existence. The difference between Dao on the 8th and 7th levels, is that Dao on the 7th level is actively engaged in the manifest cosmos, whereas Dao on the 8th level is the Dao as it is in and to itself, wholly unknowable to us.

The model is a useful presentation of disparate facts, conceptions, interpretations and simplifications. As an attempt to contract all existence, all that is, into one page, it can never succeed. Without a graphic function to accompany it, it is opaque. Not that a graphic model is necessarily less opaque, but it can give an indication of trends and tendencies which the metaphor of words on a page cannot. We would recommend a consideration of the graphic models from Helene Blavatsky [the founder of Theosophy], for they are adequate to that task, although we observe their terminology could be updated. Nevertheless, this model has some strengths.

The eighth level is necessary, of course. However, there is a useful distinction here only indicated by the "oblique" between the Dao and Pure Being, because Pure Being belongs with the origin of all that is, and the Dao is something else. It is not that the Dao is absolute transcendent consciousness. Absolute transcendent consciousness is a function and consequence of the Dao. In that sense, the Dao is the highest level and all else is subservient, being a product or consequence. Undifferentiated consciousness, which is what is meant by the phrase "absolute transcendent," is the nature of the Dao. What arises from Dao are the various levels of manifest consciousness subdivided into various levels. This is a conceptual convenience, we might add, for there are no actual subdivisions in consciousness, and they are not in their own nature differentiated in that way, such being the nature of the Dao.

The next level, the seventh, appropriately includes active Dao, active Being, because Being is a consequence of the activity of Dao. One could alternatively include that as active across both component cells in that array. With such a modification made, providing a blend between the cells of the seventh and eight levels, we suggest the model would better represent the proper connection of active Dao/active Being manifesting the cosmos.

The rest of the conception here is essentially appropriate. The exception is the term emergence, for that is more properly linked with the seventh level, the manifestation. In terms of the activity of emergence in its active quality, that should more appropriately be placed at the third level, not the second.

Q 15. Would you comment on the viability of this model with respect to your perception/ conception of the cosmos?

These conceptualisations as models have the following advantages: They allow partitioning when considering different levels of existence. That is, they suit the analytical mode of enquiry. The experiential mode of enquiry is suitably buttressed and reinforced by the analytical mode of enquiry. But these conceptualisations are better suited to a different class of individual.

In other words, there is a distinction between the analytical enquiry mode and experiential enquiry mode, which tend to be adopted by persons of different personality. It is not that one is better than the other, for the two are complementary, as are the qualities of individuals, one to another. The extent to which the terminology is shorn of references to history, and in particular devoid of the terminological associations from past centuries, including both the tantric and occult, is a means by which to bring the descriptive terminology into the twenty-first century and so leave behind those experiences and speculations from other times and places. In that sense it is useful and may function as an interpretive guide for contemporary humanity.

Its limitations are that it is far too abstract for any person to gain any sense of the complex sets of associations present within each cell of the matrix, and so would not communicate usefully to beginners. In that sense, it is a high-level ordering tool and is not to any degree appropriate for presentation to novices and beginners.

Each cell in the matrix can be construed as containing many sub-components, that is, each cell is in fact a multidimensional matrix, with millions of layers behind the top surface, as it were. So although the array model has some utility, it represents so much as to be of little value in its own right. There is no way around this.

The information coding contained within the multidimensional array is so complex it would take any individual lifetimes to appreciate it. Which is why most individuals do not approach this class of information until they are at the early mature phase of their development as an individual. Others may make approaches at earlier stages of their developmental path, but their understanding tends to be superficial. It is typically a multiple lifetime task to approach these topics.

In that sense, a useful addition to the model could be an explicit indication that it is a top-level hierarchical ordering of the complexity of all that is, with explicit explanation that each cell contains multitudes of subdivisions of information. The alert well-educated individual will quickly understand this. However, not everybody is curious regarding these factors.

11:50. In the previous recording I sensed that my current intellectual grasp of the section relating to Q 16 and beyond was insufficient. The range of reality being addressed was beyond my current capacity to easily comprehend or appreciate. I was advised to finish *The Tao of Physics,* then come back to them. The perception that has just come, however, is that there is an extent to which the model almost automatically, through its hierarchical structure, presupposes that spiritual identities are somehow separate from the manifest universe.

In an attempt to address this, we wish to focus briefly on aspects of consciousness. We note that consciousness can be equated to identity. And there are aspects of identity that are referred to in some literature as existing in the realm of "elementals." These aspects of identity are simple and small in nature, but they contain love and the Dao in their intrinsic nature.

Some of these elementals function as guiders and nurturers of components of the natural world, specifically plants and trees. Their care does not extend to insects, for they have their own inherent spiritual nature, whereas the realm of the plant has sentience, but no more. And so the elementals, who are in traditional terms, the gnome, fairy, elf and suchlike, act in love, being dedicated and observant and patient, as they nurture and attend to members of the plant kingdom.

Time is not a function of their awareness, for time pertains to physicality, not to spirituality. And they are just as constant in their attention to those aspects of the created world that they are charged to care for as any other aspect of spirituality functioning at any level.

One could view the elemental as a fine structure or local manifestation in pure Dao, with an existence that begins and ends. In that sense, elementals have a lifetime. They come into existence and die, which is the end of their manifestation. And yet, because they are a feature of spiritual life in the same sense that humanity is a feature of spiritual life, it is appropriate to include their death rate with that of the human death rate, for they are no different in significance.

We would now briefly remark on the mythology of elementals. These categories and orders of being have been observed throughout human history. Humans have projected onto them aspects of their own nature, particularly psychological characteristics, including tendencies towards greed, hatred, avarice, jealousy, and similar. This has occurred in identical fashion to those projections that were made onto the orders of beings identified as gods, orders which existed in different pantheons in various civilisations, descriptions of which in many cases are still extant.

The fact is, these projected human characteristics have never been the nature of these creatures. They have love at their core, which is expressed in their purpose. The focus of their attention, being inconceivable to, let alone observed by, other orders of identities in the manifest universe, has led human beings to identify them as being of strange and enigmatic purpose, yet mostly benign to humanity. That is true. They hold no animosity for any order of created being. As their purpose is not directed towards humanity, they possess no perceivable interest in humanity, even though perceptive humans have sometimes observed them and told stories about them. These stories subsequently developed their own momentum, acquiring projections of human emotion that humanity finds necessary and satisfying in its story-telling. But that is a feature of the stories, not of the identities referred to in the stories.

We have more to say now about this level of creation, in the sense of it being a manifestation from the Dao, but involving a different order of perception than that of the physical domain, where humans are mostly entranced by the stream of information arriving to their physical senses.

There are orders of varying magnitude among the elementals. And we point to the dance of particles as being the ebb and flow of the waters of dhamma in the vision of recent days. We remarked then that the magnification factor applicable to that vision was in the range of 5,000 to 25,000. Magnification is a capability of the spiritual perception which is not commonly recognised. Yet it is responsible for some of the strange and inexplicable perceptions recorded throughout history.

There is no limit to the magnification factor functioning in spiritual perception. It ranges from the perception of the Dao given at the beginning of this retreat, in the form of the multiverse model, down to the extremely small, applicable in the air-fog model. This variation is possible because the range of magnification produces different perceptions at different magnifications. And so, while on the spiritual level the dance of Shiva is a sophisticated description of the manifestation into recognisable entities, the additional factor of description includes the range of magnification and is useful for ordering such perceptions into appropriate ranges.

By this means one may perceive everything in the manifest universe, from the subatomic, to manifest structures in the universe, to the cosmic in scale, on to the level of the Dao. Enquiries regarding the scale of perception can always be responded to.

However, the utility of the magnification factors given earlier, of 5,000 to 25,000, is meaningless unless there is a reference point. We offer as a reference point the dimensions of the human – not in their physical form, but in their auric analogue. The structure of that auric analogue can be examined down to the level of the minute. Its composition within its associated soul group can be represented in the same terms.

And so, because this is a description aimed at the adult human, we take a two metre value as representative. This is naturally approximate and generalised, but it provides a connecting link between the dimensions attributed to spiritual identities without magnification by offering a reference point of one, if one may assign that value to it.

Accordingly, elementals typically range in size from 0.1 to 200 of such units. Perceptions of scale outside this range therefore do not involve perceptions of elementals.

We choose this range of perception purely for convenience, as a conceptual ordering tool for descriptive purposes. It has no other purpose.

Next we wish to comment on the manifestation from the spiritual into the physical. There are many categories of this manifestation. Almost all of them are known. They range in size from the subatomic to the cosmic, that is, the arising of the universe, to speak only of this one.

The fundamental reason for the manifestation and existence of this particular universe is that its purpose is experimental. The universe's manifold physical forms and life-forms generate multiple dimensions of information that becomes encoded into its structure. Understanding is acquired when that information is returned to the level of the Dao, ultimate consciousness.

The collection of that information is via the group soul. That is the point of the process of assigning multiple lifetimes to each created fragment of the group soul, then collecting and combining information, followed by distilling out repetition and redundancy so that a coherent understanding, averaged across all group souls, can be transferred to the Dao.

We decline to nominate any further description of components, or offer any further description of aggregate forms above the level of the group soul. They exist, but for this delineation of the structure, and explicitly to avoid the degradation of this description into an opportunity for worship of imagined deity, we will not do so.

Not that we are intrinsically against worship. It functions to focus the constituent aspects of a life towards a positive ideal. That has value to the extent that it is a positive ideal that embodies loving-nature. Of course, humans have the freedom to incorporate other elements, or substitute completely different elements, into their formulation of the object of worship.

However, this is intended to be a description favouring the rational over the adorational. As such, it is designed to be suitable for the time and within the civilisation in which it has emerged. During other eras such descriptions have favoured different aspects and elements, in accordance with the values perceived as necessary for survival during those times.

CHAPTER SEVEN

Interlude: Three

[A one week break in the retreat occurred, as Peter was required to return home to fulfil various engagements, including attending a regular meditation group.]

12 May

20:15. After arriving back at Matapaua, I fitted the new stove oven lamp and organised a light noodle meal. I then recorded a CD to my USB music stick and played it to prove the system works. Now to sit a while, then sleep.

We come on this occasion in order to assuage any guilt or anxiety about the unwillingness or the unfitness to proceed in carrying out this task of answering Keith Hill's questions. There are no impediments. It only takes time. If it takes longer, it does not matter. The time frame for the effective dispersal of the received results vastly outweighs the time frame for the reception of those materials.

So it does not matter if there is one day here or there gained or missed. It is completely unimportant. Therefore relax! The task of accumulating and processing this material is not trivial. Relax! There is no necessity to adopt a sense of urgency related to this material. Relax! The essential condition in order to receive the material is in a condition of relaxation. Therefore relax!

It is not your fault that it did not come yesterday or last year. Given its implications, and the breadth of frameworks addressed, this material is more than sufficient to occupy the minds of most individuals for their entire lifetime. It has taken half of yours in order to produce what has already been done. So from this point forwards enjoy the process and do not feel burdened by it.

13 May

09:02. I slept well. It's a beautiful day here, with sunshine, calm sea and no wind. The rabbit ran, but the oyster catcher slept on, standing on one leg with its beak buried in its feathers. I have company in the next house but one, identified by footprints in the wet sand, partly obliterated by the last high tide. I'm feeling more peaceful again now. Will spend today winding down even further.

11:33. Have sat again, during which I received the exhortation to immerse myself in the material by thoroughly re-reading it, thereby confronting my ignorance and the need to transcend it. Chilled now with the approach of spirit:

We need to know you care enough to confront yourself. That constitutes the question to which we can then respond. It must be personal rather than just responding to someone else's questions. Your life has become comfortable as a result of state support. That is only the body's needs. Where is your curiosity? You used to be so curious!

17:14. I thought of going for a walk, but realised all I wanted to do was sleep. I slept two ninety minute cycles, then woke with an insistent: "Now walk! To the top of the hill and back! Every day!"

I did and found it mildly taxing. I have no appetite and find myself wanting to live on my fat for a few days. I then re-read this compilation.

14 May

08.42. Slept well for approximately ten hours. The weather is closing in, with a northerly wind and heavy cloud. I read Fritjof Capra's *The Tao of Physics*. As an introduction to the essentials of physics and eastern mysticism it is highly relevant to the visions I've had so far here.

And we would take you further. Be seated with your recorder.

The harmonies observed between the world views of the mystic and the scientist, as promulgated in scientific literature, along with the availability of mystical literature translated into modern English, make it possible to demonstrate the accord between the opposed worldviews of physics and mysticism. Yet even the perception that they are opposed worldviews is false. This is because, as Capra had the insight and wisdom to specify, they are complementary views of the one phenomenon. We would emphasise the nature of the phenomenon as being one. That is, it is predetermined to be conceptually and preternaturally unitary. And we here introduce the concept of the preternatural into this discussion and monologue.

The natural and the preternatural, that is, the ordinary and what is beyond the ordinary, are complementary. Your capacity to see into both domains has generated an intrinsic respect for both physical and spiritual perception, derived from direct cognition via non-ordinary channels.

However, we would emphasise that what is perceived through both natural and preternatural channels is illusory, in the sense that they are constructs of the mind and the sensory perceptual systems which cognise them. We can do nothing about this, for we are speaking to an embodied individual of the type homo sapiens sapiens. Therefore the limitations of the organic brain and its associated perceptual systems, of its energetic foundational structure, if we may phrase it in that way, lead to a certain view of the nature of unitary reality which is essentially a product of the observing organism. Other non-human species, which contain or comprise different perceptual systems, would not describe reality in the same way.

So we emphasise that what is seen is a product of the observing human being who perceives and attempts to relate their perceptions to their particular worldview and sensory systems. Changing any one of those aspects necessarily changes the result, as it is a product of the design of the organism itself.

From outside the organism, that is, from the perspective of the disembodied state, one is not constrained by the limitations of the physical organism and its perceptual systems. Therefore between one disembodied identity and species and another there is greater potential for harmony between their descriptions of existence.

A necessary precondition for ascribing validity to the preternatural perspective is the existence, prior to embodiment, of the human identity in a disembodied state. This brings us to the distinction between the perspectives obtained via the two complementary states, embodied and disembodied. One could argue that the disembodied state contains the greater percentage of mystical intuitions, because perception is not clouded or made more complex by input from the human body's organic perceptual systems. To that degree, the sense of unity between the two sets of natural and preternatural observations is rather easier to obtain when disembodied than when in a body.

This makes disembodied perceptions somewhat more reliable than embodied perceptions. However, disembodied perceptions are accessed by those in the embodied state rarely and ephemerally. This makes it unlikely that the perspective offered by disembodied perceptions will ever be granted full legitimacy in the natural human world.

Nonetheless, we beg to differ. Due to the innate illusory nature of perceptions of unitary reality by embodied humans, we argue for the greater intrinsic reliability of the disembodied mystical viewpoint. We know, or at least predict, that there will be few adherents to this perspective due to the small proportion of mystics in the world population. That does not invalidate our point of view. But we recognise it is limited to the initiated few, which thereby minimises its influence.

That seems to be that. Immediately chilled again now.

We come again to continue this monologue, in accordance with the articles of association and prior agreements, communicating across time, space and population density, if we may phrase it that way.

It is not necessary to imbibe, quaff or swallow all we say. It is presented entirely for evaluation by those humans who care to do so. Its worth is not intrinsically greater than any similar series of pronouncements made at any other time or in any other place. It is a monologue suitable for this time and this place, during this period of intelligent discussion among intelligent humans on this small planet. It is irrelevant to any dialogue with other species or even, one could argue, to a condition in which all participants were disembodied, especially when those participants are naive in their experience of physicality. Contextualised in that way, we continue.

The articles which we wish to discuss at this point transcend everything conveyed or construed prior to this point in our monologue series. Therefore some rather unusual conditions will need to be facilitated within this organism in order to ensure its safety and to enable the recording to continue. Accordingly, we will take a few moments to disestablish this organism and its history from the boundaries to which it ordinarily adheres.

I've been advised to lie down in order to facilitate this experience, so the body can more easily relax into submissiveness while I'm out of it.

Lying down now, I sense that the intention is to achieve an out of body experience and a dialogue transmitted from that perspective into this recording device. I have no idea how long this will take. But I feel it necessary to leave the recorder on and assist the process by intending to ascend on the hara level. I'm feeling energy surges and activation in the ajna.

It's unnecessary to comment further.

I experienced repeated inner invitations to "Come out now," but seemed not to. I wonder what fear – or laziness – held me back? For thirty-five minutes slow quiet breathing was recorded, but not much else.

11:06. I've just finished, finally, *The Tao of Physics*, with reminders of David Bohm and the implicate order and an intuition that it is identified with the electrospiritual domain. That's probably significant. I noticed the usual chill and was informed that they are always around me, that they love me and look out for me. Well, that's nice. And, I think, sufficient for a foundation of security and identity.

15:37. I've sat again in order to proceed to the next thing, whatever it may be. While sitting I sought to investigate the source of the conjectured fear and/or laziness in the earlier exercise. I've found an internal infantile self, frightened by noises in the night, perhaps the result of intrusion from adults or siblings or some such. I reassured it, obtained the expression of its feelings, and identified it accordingly. I then put it into my heart and absolved it of further responsibility.

I next addressed the resistance that I described as laziness. I think there is a convergence of those two emotions and activities. I seized that aspect within myself, even though it attempted to elude me, and I brought it up close. It had the appearance of something roundish, vaguely ellipsoidal or slug-like – not really, but that kind of shape. I then slit it open and out came fluttering birds!

I could make no sense of that until I remembered that one of my tasks as a child was to feed the chickens. I became embittered and resistant about doing that task, and either stopped doing it or negotiated to be rid of it. I see that as a root of the intransigence, the unwillingness to do as requested. So that was the resented chore, one of many, and presumably a root of – in Michael terms – the negative chief feature. Except it would not be actually the chief feature, but rather a corollary or associate.

Interestingly, I now perceive on my left a somewhat snarling identity, as if saying, "I hope you enjoy your compliance, you fool!" Or words to that effect.

I seized that aspect. It seemed to be a combination of malevolent low animal cunning, as represented by insolent eyes and refusal – refusal to act, refusal to know, refusal to love, refusal to comply. I identify it, in Buddhist terms, as a defilement, and asked that it be taken away and destroyed. Help came from the right, as usual. And whereas its natural location was low in relation to my own self, it was taken up high, or I projected it and held it there. I then untangled it and held it up to the light.

That is merely the latest in a long series of such inner tendencies and sub-personalities, or so one could describe them, which I've hunted down and eliminated one by one since 1990, using these techniques.

As a result there seems to be greater inner clarity, to a greater depth, than before, as if a layer of contrary impulse had evaporated.

15 May

07:08. This morning I've finished *Eat When Hungry* by Joanne Fedler, with its theme of journey and loss and finding home internally. Straight away chilled:

> We wish on this occasion to cement the gains made in understanding. Take time out to review the questions and re-read highlights of the text. We will direct your focus of attention.

I did that. I then received a suggestion to walk to relieve my sore seat. I went outside and realised I could photograph the hillside rock formation I have been mentally imaging as a figure, and that I could do so from the house deck instead of climbing the hillside. So I got the camera on its tripod, set it up, and just as I was about to take the picture against the dark sky, the clouds parted to

CHAPTER EIGHT

A Proposed Model
of Reality (Continued)

Q 16. With respect to level 2, to my mind it embeds various tendencies in the matter and energy of level 1, giving everything in that level direction. One clear tendency is the propensity for simpler forms to become more complex, giving rise to growth, emergence and evolution. So matter is not a blank canvas, governed entirely by chance. Certain tendencies are innate in the manifest cosmos. My model suggests that these tendencies emanate from level 6. Your thoughts on this?

The issue in question is the discussion concerning the degree to which emanation of intention from level 6 in the Keith Hill model has anything at all to do with the manifestation of complexity of forms, function and life from simpler forms, function and life, resulting in growth, emergence and evolution. Our perspective on this question, and it is a complex response because it is a complex question, is as follows.

First, we would say that there are levels of order. Manifestations of growth and the development in complexity within the manifest universe are a natural function of the tendencies in-built at that level.

So it is not that there is on-going emanation from the model's level 6 to influence the outcomes of the model's level 2. Rather, the conditions were initially defined. Then, as a consequence of the minimisation of encoded energy within structure, natural tendencies towards accretion, clustering, and spontaneous organisation manifested because they are features of the patterns intrinsically present within the design. The result is that these varieties of systematic ordering will occur spontaneously, or apparently spontaneously, due to the tendencies in-built within level 2.

To that extent, it is not necessary to postulate ongoing interference, to put it that way, or influence, or the injection of energy or order, or any similar factor, because those tendencies are already constructed within the rules of association. The innate tendency is to find optimal simplicity of complex nature.

That is sufficient as an explanation. This information is now well known and it is related to the arising of spontaneous order out of chaos. That process is what is being referred to here.

Questions 17 to 19 were answered fully, but I mismanaged the recording and captured none of it. Instead, I got a long quiet period in audio record!

It is difficult to stay sufficiently present so as to manage the recording well, yet stay sufficiently out of the way to render the discourse.

I sat until I felt calm again, then prepared fruitcake mix, went for a walk on the beach, and sat in the sun a while. I then mixed the cake. It is baking now. It's much easier to see what's going on in the oven since I fitted the new lamp. I will walk up the hill when it's done and cooling. Then have coffee and cake.

The sliding kitchen door works easily now, which is useful to keep the heat in the living area. I have brought a few CDs of music generally in the meditation style, including Chinese Buddhist.

Finally, I asked for a redelivery of the non-captured questions and got a very loving affirmation. Nothing is lost, not even part of it. Am I not human and fallible?

I've felt directed to lie down. I assumed this is another opportunity to conduct the exercise which was unsuccessful last night, of exiting the body, during which I discovered fear and resistance. On consulting my inner motivation, I requested all fear to become present. I then felt pain in my right wrist. What came to mind was another time and place, when I was suspended or chained by the wrists. This was during a period in a torture chamber, where I was rendered insane due to the procedures carried out on my body. Having acknowledged that, the pain went.

I understand that at that time the soul departed, leaving only a compliant remnant with wide blue vacant eyes, a plaything of the torturer in which he demonstrated that compliance to others and wondered at it. The fact that pain was in my right hand causes me to wonder if that was a factor in my left-handedness as a child.

I've just heard, "Turn the recorder on," coming from the right. "We invite your exit now." But I wonder how to do that best?

19:16. Out-of-body experience attempt three. Duration sixty-one minutes. I don't know what happened in this last recording. I think I just went to sleep! But I've been encouraged to try again so here we go ...

I listened to the complete recording of the first session. Apart from my initial voiced thoughts, I heard only quiet breathing. I believe I slept throughout most of the time. Or at least I could not differentiate from the recording whether I was sleeping or doing anything else. I remembered nothing at the recording end, so assume I merely slept.

We come on this occasion in order to respond to Question 17.

Q 17. With respect to level 3, the physical realm, what strikes me most is that, first, it is filled with different orders of organisation and, second, that a higher order of organisation cannot be predicted, or even conceived of, by a lower order. For example, a rock consists of a particular ordering of crystalline molecules. A flower is a higher order of organisation. It grows and responds to its environment. An ant is a higher order. It grows, responds to its environment, and exists in a hive within a strict social ordering. Human beings exist at an even higher order of species organisation again, responding to their environment in very complex ways, as well as possessing an introspective ability. A flower can have no concept, couldn't even imagine, the social organisation of an ant. Neither can an ant have any awareness of the complexity of human ordering. It appears highly possible that, on the physical level, there are even higher orders of organisation that we can have no concept of. For example, various thinkers over the ages have suggested that the Sun and Earth are consciousness beings. Your thoughts?

It is true that there are many orders of organisation among humans, as well as among lower-order organisms. The prime purpose of the orders of organisation is to discern the capacity for life in appropriate environmental niches. Environmental niches exist in various places around the Earth, for short or long periods, within the random dispersal of order and disorder in the physical domain. The environmental niches themselves are a product of the multiplexed tendencies to create order out of chaos.

When a suitable environmental niche is identified from that level where responsibility is taken for seeding such niches with appropriate organisms, those organisms are created, or modified from preexisting stock, and distributed in a way that enables a breeding population to become established. They are then left to their own devices. Those that survive do; those that do not, don't. There is no particular concern over either outcome. It is the relationship between the characteristics of the niche and the surviving organism that matter and is recorded. To that extent, there is no necessity for communication between orders of organisms.

The exceptions, of course, are other species that form long-term associations with humanity – we focus on the human because this communication is with a sentient human being. Obviously ants do not, sea slugs do not, nor do most wild species. Therefore, there is no need for the capacity for inter-species communication to be explicitly built into these combinations of species. The exception would be the capacity to read body language between related orders of species – hoofed mammals, for example. Another general exception is between predator and prey. And, on some occasions, the subtle level of communication commonly called mind-reading and telepathy that occurs between companion animals and humans, or between one human and another.

Incidentally, it is tempting to assign telepathy to the quality of communication between a disembodied human and an embodied human, but such is not the case. In that case, what actually occurs is subtle communication using the auric channel. And, of course, it is only the individual human who is sufficiently aware and alert through that channel who possesses those particular qualities of perception.

Regarding the question as to whether solar bodies and the Sun are consciousness beings, the answer is no. These are simple attributions on the part of the evolving human, made in an attempt to explain behaviour in the physical environment. In this case, intention is attributed to the beneficial processes of fostering life, processes which are actually a product of design that creates and fills environmental niches. No more than that.

Q 18. I assume that the same principle of orders of organisation applies at level five, in relation to the spiritual realm. We human beings have a spiritual part and we participate with existence on this level, existing there between incarnations. But there must be orders of spiritual organisation, presumably both higher and lower than us. Your thoughts?

It is true that at the level designated in the model as level 5, relating to spiritual organisation and associated stratum, there are orders of being higher than the group soul. It is our specific intention not to give any detail whatsoever about such orders of organisation. Yes, they exist. No, we will not describe them.

The point, and we have said this in other places, is to avoid the worship of imagined deity. There is no validity in this, let alone value.

It is much more appropriate that each individual come to understand the relationship between themselves in their current incarnation and their higher mind, including the set of prior personalities constituting the higher mind, and communicate with that level. Individuals may further understand that they are part of a larger set of individuals, most of whom they will never know. Which does not matter.

What is being constructed is a repository of their experience, both personal and group, in order to convey it to higher levels again, which they will also never know. The collected experience produces the outcome of this experiment.

The search after purpose is best focused towards engaging, on a conscious level, with the individual life purpose, rather than subsuming the life purpose into ignorance and mere subconscious awareness. If the individual life purpose is consciously discovered and engaged, even if only at the life's conclusion, then there will be a sense of the life having been worth living, or enduring, or celebrating, as the case may be.

The attribution of god-like status to the higher self is simply silly. A more useful result comes from developing a detailed appreciation through ongoing communication, as in the case with this individual – although this does not mean that any individual necessarily needs to focus on establishing their life purpose and understanding their higher mind, because there are many other intentions possible for a given life. In the context of this discussion, it is only that this task is the life purpose of this particular individual. Nevertheless, it is worth generalising. And as will be recalled, this is also an opportunity to provide a reminder to those who forget because they asked for one.

In terms of the orders of organisation on the spiritual level, but at a different level from the human, and in a lower rather than a higher range on the scale of agapé, we would point to the previous discussion concerning the realm of the elementals. They occur at a range of approximately 15 to

25 on the agapé scale. Accordingly, they can be construed to be adjacent in nature, and able to be perceived under appropriate conditions. And, of course, their have own purposes, which are focused towards their concerns and not towards the human.

Q. 19. Level 4 is the realm of thought. Thought functions as passive, active and reconciling. Thought is passive when we use it to react to what is going on around us. Thought is active when we use it to create and explore the possibilities in our lives, and in activities such as telekinesis. And thought is reconciling when it brings together disparate levels and situations and resolves them, such as ethical thinking and ideas that lift us out of where we are to a higher level of understanding. For now, what is your response to the function of thought in this model?

Thought is primarily a level of inner functioning or inner communication between different aspects of the mind, and occasionally between one mind and another. The qualities of thought are the point of discussion in this section.

Thought does not occupy a particular level. Thought is a tool for conveying understanding, information, appreciation, dynamics, explanation, analysis. More than anything else, it is an instrument for communicating between an individual's different aspects. Perhaps most importantly, the function of thought is within each of the higher mind and the lower mind, and between the two.

Secondarily, thought is utilised for communication within the lower mind. This involves processing information received from beyond the lower mind and its brain in order to form effective social organisation, social structure, social networks, procreative bonds, and dominance relationships. All of these affect survival in the physical domain.

In addition, the alert individual utilises a variety of abstractions in order to convey information, to store information within themselves, and to communicate that effectively with others. None of this presupposes that there is anything abstract or concrete in thought as a tool. It is better regarded as a medium by which to process information.

Accordingly, it is appropriate to designate a level in the model that directly addresses thought because of its information processing capacity. The consequence of thought may involve emotion or survival. It can also be supernal. This occurs when an individual successfully communicates with higher aspects of its own identity, or with other disembodied identities higher than itself in the spiritual domain. It thereby gains access to a richer context within which to exist and survive.

When there is sufficient fluidity and depth of communication between all levels within a particular identity, the contribution that individual makes to their society and culture may have particular relevance. Most individuals do not achieve that level of fluidity and capacity. However, this does not matter in most instances, given that the predilection for social relations is so important to survival and procreation.

The significance of thought, and a designated level for that capacity in the given model is sufficient, although it is to be understood as representative but not fully descriptive. It is a pointer to the significance of information flows throughout all orders of existence and created being. That is the sense in which it is representative rather than distributed across the entire set of levels.

[This next question has largely already been answered. Nonetheless, I include it here as it has stimulated previous responses.]

Q 20. Levels 6, 7 and 8 are an attempt to get my head around the higher order of organisation that I assume exists beyond the level 5 spiritual realm. Scientists consider that for the physical universe to be stable and to have created conditions for life to evolve a tuning of certain numbers was required. Cosmologist Martin Rees has identified six numbers as key, for example the ratio of the strength of the electrical forces that bind sub-atomic particles into atoms divided by the force of gravity between them. If these six numbers were different the universe would not have evolved into what it is. This gives rise to questions regarding the relationship of what I am calling levels 6, 7 and 8, and what scientists would call pre-Big Bang conditions. There are three possible positions regarding these numbers or patterns.

(1) These numbers were the result of pure chance. They appear by us to be right, and even to be preordained, because if these numbers were not the way they are, human beings would not exist.

(2) Some scientists have a problem with (1) because the likelihood of these numbers being "just right" is incredibly slim. In order to increase the likelihood of chance generating these pre-Big Bang conditions they postulate that there may have been a massive

number of Big Bangs, with a huge variety of key numbers and ratios embedded in them, which created a massive number of universes. Most failed because the numbers didn't work together to create a stable universe. Our universe was one of these vast numbers of universes that actually "worked". However, the problem with (2) is that there is no evidence that this occurred. And there is no way of testing for the existence of alternative universes. So it remains pure speculation. Instead, another explanation is offered.

(3) This is an evolving model. It postulates that over a vast period of time a huge number of universes have predated our universe, and as each collapsed certain values were retained that subsequently manifested in the next version of the universe. So the universe gradually evolved over a period of lifetimes, in effect seeding itself with embedded values that worked to generate stability, while those values that did not were discarded. Over a vast period of time, through chance combinations the universe eventually "tuned" itself into its current form.

(4) Alternatively, religious people postulate that a super-natural, transcendent being, called God, selected the numbers then initiated the Big Bang. In terms of my model, this God would be at level 8, "ruling" the other levels.

(5) Finally, there is the possibility that these eight levels are packed into each other as a whole existent. But rather than being a ladder of levels, each level includes and transcends the level below it. This means that level 1 is at the centre and level 8 embraces all the others. This model allows for the whole being a conscious entity, with consciousness being the constituent that binds the entire structure together. Consciousness plays with chance, chance allows for choice, and the entire entity is evolving. So there is no "God" sitting above, pulling strings, deciding how things should be. Nor does the universe consist of mindless matter functioning within laws of probability that arose by chance. Instead, there is an organically evolving totality, that we exist within, that is conscious, and is mind bogglingly larger than human beings can conceive.

Personally, hypothesis (5) appeals to me, as it explains the preordained numbers, selected by the consciousness existing at levels 6, 7 and 8, but that consciousness is innately and inseparably a part of what is. Your thoughts?

In recent days we have provided a multiverse model which is intended to provide a context within which Question 20 may be answered in a systematic way. Our perspective favours sub-point 5, as it offers an approximate description of the model we have presented. That vision involves a set of universes constructed across a range of parameter values that were then set in motion in order to explore the consequences. The multiverse model assumes that knowledge is necessarily preexistent, that intention utilises knowledge to create the experimental conditions, that a range of different conditions are selected, and that a particular collection of alternate values are explored within a small number of specific parameters.

The number of universes can be specified as relatively small, five to ten. The exact number is unimportant. The exploration involves opportunities for the creation of environmental niches, with curiosity as to the outcome.

Other orders of spiritual being were, and are, given the opportunity to exercise their creativity in the formation of life forms appropriate to the available environmental niches. There is no certainty as to which niche can or cannot be exploited. And there is only a probability of survival as a result of matching a particular organism to a specific niche. Therefore the opportunity is both for the initial seeding of environmental niches with organisms, and for reseeding when it is experimentally determined what parameters of organism capacities are required in order to best exploit a given range of niches. There is also provision for recognition of the development of sentience and intelligence with the creation of a container via which that intelligence may gather information about the circumstances in which it survives and thrives, and the conditions under which it does so and under which it does not. There is also provision for the retrieval of that information in an ongoing way.

The optimal outcome is for the experiences of multiple lives to be accumulated at the group soul level, with the understanding that that is the repository for the information.

What happens after that will not be described. Nor may the orders of organisation be spoken about in detail. We have previously specified that our explanation will be confined to this particular universe. This communication is with homo sapiens sapiens, and will be confined to this particular planet and to the orders of identity with which homo sapiens sapiens comes into association. As we have stated, there are other orders of being besides these. They will not be described.

We have indicated that the species will come to an end with the final phases of existence of the local star. If one considers life to be only physical, then that can appear to be a condition causing desperation to escape. On the other hand, if it is understood that the identity is spiritual first, foremost and always, then naturally one escapes. All that occurs is that a particular animal species ceases to procreate. The generated identities have already gone. Therefore there is no concomitant sense of loss. Rather, there is celebration at the satisfying conclusion to a successful species.

CHAPTER NINE

On the Nature
of Consciousness

17 May

Yesterday afternoon I walked to Opito, getting only slightly wet on the way back. I saw three youngish women walking on the beach with dogs and a pram, so I guess that a few people actually live there. Contractors were cleaning the road drains and catch pits along Matapaua and Blackjack Roads. Just as well, as it has rained heavily here, causing washouts. My legs know the distance now and object. Slept well to recover.

> We come in order to respond to the questions at hand so as to facilitate a rapid exit from this location to the home of this individual in this incarnation. A situation will arise there requiring attention within the next three days, so we intend to complete responses to the questions today.

Humanity currently has two main definitions of consciousness. The first is the materialist view that consciousness is identical with mind, and mind is a function of the working of the physical brain. So when the body and its brain die, mind disappears, and individual consciousness ceases to exist.

The second is the spiritual view. This is that consciousness is non-material and non-physical, and that an individual spirit enters the body at birth (or thereabouts) and leaves the body when the body dies.

Both the scientific and spiritual views of consciousness are concerned with human consciousness, because that is all we can imagine as existing. However, as is clear in your two books through Peter you consider human consciousness to be a subset of a wider range of forms of consciousnesses than human beings ordinarily recognise. The following questions are designed to elucidate your view in the context of current human knowledge.

Q 21. My first question is, what is your definition of consciousness in and of itself, separate from particular levels or manifestations?

The intuition that consciousness arises is an accurate one in the sense that consciousness is passive in its condition of mere alertness or sentience. The arising of consciousness is a manifestation on multiple levels.

The idea that consciousness is an attribute of some thing is incorrect. It is an attribute of some process. The process at its most fundamental level is the Dao. Consciousness is a process of Dao that is subject to diffusion into other levels of manifestation.

Consciousness is a distributed function. The *observer* has intellect and purpose because the Dao generates those qualities. The penetration of the Dao is universal. That is, the Dao is everywhere and everywhen. Therefore the engendered consciousness is everywhere and everywhen.

How generation occurs is that Dao is focused, if one can imagine that process, into a node of consciousness. This node is a function of Dao. The function can be on a variety of levels. Consciousness is in every manifest being as well as in every unmanifest being – and we use the term manifest in the sense of "rendered into the domain of the physical." The result is that a variety of manifest beings, on the level of species, have intellect and purpose to varying degrees.

The awareness of an ant is an example of a node of consciousness, being the specific function of an organic brain. Therefore consciousness may be viewed as a product of the activity of processing physical sense data. In the same way, consciousness may also be viewed as a function of the processing of non-physical sense data.

So we make the distinction between the generation of consciousness at the level of the human brain, that is, the function of mind associated with the organic brain, and the simultaneous but separate function of consciousness in the unmanifest and spiritual higher mind, the latter being a function that includes identity, intellect, purpose, focused awareness, observational capacity, and an array of categories of action which relate specifically to purpose.

And so there needs to be a new definition, or at least a new distinction, between the generation of Dao as spiritual consciousness and the generation of biological mind as consciousness. In the latter, consciousness is the product of a functioning information processing unit, in the form of an organic nerve centre, whether that nerve centre is primitive, as in the case of an ant, or advanced, as with the human brain.

Accordingly, we propose that the term intellect be subdivided into the distinct terms of bio-intellect and Dao-intellect. This will enable greater clarity to be brought to this discussion of consciousness.

The nature of the Dao is to have consciousness. Consciousness is an intrinsic and fundamental attribute of the Dao. Distributed unmanifest consciousness on the level of the Dao is determined and focussed into a node of intellect and purpose. This is the activity of Dao-consciousness: to generate a node of consciousness, then to utilise that function. In a similar way, Dao on the level of physical form manifests a node of bio-consciousness in order to generate bio-intellect and purpose.

This distinction between Dao-intellect and bio-intellect is a means by which to somewhat more accurately define, delimit and differentiate the realms of consciousness being discussed here.

One difficulty with the god-centred world view is that there has been insufficient differentiation between categories of intellect. We hope that these differentiated terms will allow every incarnate person to acquire a greater understanding of the breadth of both manifested and unmanifested consciousness that comprise the domain of Dao.

Specifically addressing Question 28 then: The definition of consciousness we have just provided is that it is dual, being differentiated by level. Consciousness comes from, and is a node of, Dao. It functions on two levels: the manifest and the unmanifest.

Q 22. My reading of ancient spiritual texts suggests that either: (a) consciousness is a fundamental aspect of Dao, i.e. consciousness is Dao, or (b) consciousness is a function or manifestation of Dao.

Regarding this distinction, the ancient Indian meditators suggested in the Upanishads *and* Bhagavad Gita *that consciousness is identical with Brahman, the Absolute, and that human consciousness is a portion of, or participates in, Brahman. (I understand Brahman to be another word for Dao.) The implication of this view is that, as Brahman is everywhere, consciousness must be a fundamental substrate of the cosmos, in the same way that energy and mass are fundamental to, and inseparable from, the physical universe. Your view on this?*

Consciousness is both a function and a manifestation of Dao. It is a fundamental aspect of Dao. Nevertheless, it is not that consciousness is Dao. This is a subtle and important distinction, referred to in the Upanishads and Bhagavad Gita, where it is stated that consciousness is identical with Brahman and that human consciousness participates in Brahman. And, in this context, it is valid to assume that Brahman is another word for Dao.

To that degree, consciousness is a fundamental substrate of the manifest physical universe, being a function generated within it. If one presupposes that consciousness is a product of a physical information processing centre, such as a brain, then it is just as valid to identify bio-consciousness as it is to identify Dao-consciousness. The function is the same in each, that being to process information. The word consciousness must be differentiated in this manner to avoid confusion.

Q. 23. Is consciousness eternal? I ask this because if consciousness is a function of Dao, it will come and go, rise and fall, and therefore have a life span. But if consciousness is a fundamental aspect of Dao, because Dao always is, so will consciousness always exist.

With consciousness defined and delineated into bio-consciousness and Dao-consciousness, it is now possible to disentangle the question of whether consciousness is eternal. In the sense that consciousness is a function of Dao, it will come and go. It is variable and can be thought of as having a life span. In its unmanifest form it is eternal, because Dao is eternal. However, it is confusing to even apply the term eternal to the Dao, precisely because the word implies viewing the question from the perspective of the time-bound realm. Flexibility of perspective is essential in order to make the distinction clear.

From the perspective of Dao-consciousness, eternality does not apply because there is no time. From the perspective of the manifest universe, in which time exists, Dao-consciousness is appropriately considered to be eternal, in contrast to bio-consciousness which is not eternal, because it is a product of the functioning brain, whatever kind of brain that may be.

CHAPTER TEN

On Orders of Conscious Beings

The following questions focus on how consciousness manifests in particular forms of living beings, beings which possess different orders of organisation and levels of awareness. I assume that consciousness manifests in particular species, and that these species possess different orders of perceptual, motor, emotional, intellectual, social and spiritual organisation. These differing orders of organisation naturally give rise to different levels of awareness. Thus, on Earth, plants, insects, mammals, and human beings are each different orders of biological organisation, and each possesses a different level of awareness.

It also seems reasonable to assume that Earth is not the only place in the cosmos where consciousness manifests in living creatures. In your books through Peter you suggest that there are many different orders of consciousness existing throughout the cosmos, many of which do not exist as embodied beings. So the following questions fall into four categories, to do with terrestrial orders of living beings, both embodied and disembodied, and non-terrestrial orders of living beings, also embodied and disembodied. I'll begin with non-terrestrial beings.

There is much misinformation, misunderstanding, misinterpretation of experience, attribution to false or unreliable levels of experience, and general confusion about the factors under discussion in Questions 24 to 39. However, we will endeavour to bring clarity to these distinctions to the best that we are able at this time.

NON-TERRESTRIAL EMBODIED CONSCIOUS BEINGS

Q 24. Are embodied beings common throughout the Milky Way Galaxy and, by extension, throughout the universe?

Yes, of course this is the case. The fact that few are in evidence to the human does not imply, given humanity's limited range of observation, that there are no other species in evidence within the universe, particularly non-terrestrial embodied conscious beings.

There are, however, significant records of encounters with such non-terrestrial beings, which are validated by this comment, even though accounts of these encounters are subject to the usual exaggerations, often being full of fear responses and tending to impute negative or destructive intention to non-terrestrial beings.

However, we do also note that some non-terrestrial species exhibit a willingness to invade human personal space and being integrity, as this particular individual has registered, with some so-called non-terrestrial beings having proved willing to invade the integrity of his body-space.

Q 25. We assume biologies are carbon-based. Is this the case through the cosmos?

It is true that the existence within a carbon-based biology naturally tends to engender the expectation that other embodied beings are of a similar nature. Of course, that is a falsely confined perspective. There are other bases for embodiment. While we decline to specify such things, we will affirm that there are bases for embodiment which are not a construction from organic carbon.

Q 26. Because our biology is sophisticated in relation to other species, we assume that biological complexity equates with levels of consciousness. Your thoughts?

It is false to assume that the human is the highest level of consciousness, or the most complex organism, or the most complex mind in existence. It is also false to equate levels of consciousness with biological complexity. There is a tendency to associate more complex consciousness with more complex biology. But that is not necessarily the case.

Accordingly, we would make you aware of the distinction between complexity of organism and complexity of associated mind. In general terms, where the complexity of bio-consciousness indicates an organism's complexity, that complexity indicates nothing regarding the Dao-consciousness inhabiting that organism.

It needs to be recognised that just as varieties of different Dao-consciousnesses are associated with different organisms and their bio-consciousnesses, this applies equally to non-terrestrial species, where bio-consciousness is associated with, but not conditional on, a high level of Dao-consciousness. We cannot say more than this without discussing other non-terrestrial species in detail, which is not our brief.

Q 27. Are stars conscious beings?

We have already addressed this question earlier. We affirm that stars, like planets, and like all groupings of matter brought by gravity into association, one particle with another, are no more than that. This is not to say that they could not be conscious. But they are not.

The function of agglomerations of matter is to provide environmental niches for the development of species so that information may be acquired in the ways we have already outlined. Within that scenario there is no requirement for the agglomerations of matter to have independent life or to be conscious to any degree.

The belief that such agglomerations are conscious is a misattribution of the relationship between life forms and their associated Dao-consciousness. This misattribution results when perceivers see that they are surrounded by a network of Dao-consciousnesses, and they then wrongly attribute consciousness to the agglomerated body of matter that provides the environmental niches which serve to develop bio-consciousness.

It is this misattribution that has generated the belief, and we assert a false belief, that the matter comprising and giving rise to the environmental niches contain consciousness. We therefore assert that stars are not conscious beings.

NON-TERRESTRIAL DISEMBODIED CONSCIOUS BEINGS

Q 28. What is the proportion of embodied beings to disembodied beings?

Although there is little benefit in responding to this question, we assert that the ratio of embodied beings to disembodied beings is small.

Q 29. Do all disembodied beings incarnate in bodies at some stage during their life cycles?

In general, yes. But not invariably.

Q 30. Where do disembodied beings exist? What is their habitat? In my previous model I suggested level 5 as a spiritual realm in which disembodied beings exist. I assume that different levels of organisation exist on this level. Is this the case?

Referring to the Keith Hill model and level 5 as a spiritual realm in which embodied beings exist: the model is just a model. It has no reality in itself. Therefore it is inappropriate to specify that level 5 on that model is in any sense a level on which disembodied beings exist.

The domain of the disembodied is extensive. We have earlier referred to a model of the astral domain being a partial location for the existence of disembodied life. It is inappropriate to pronounce on the extent to which it is partial, except to say that it is miniscule in relation to the non-astral domain, that is, to the clear light domain whereby ordinary individuals cast from the Dao have their being. In that sense, level 5 can be equated with not only the astral domain and the associated model representing that which we have already given, but also with the entire realm of the clear light, of which no information may be given.

We apologise that it is not possible to respond to Question 30 to the extent the questioner requests.

Q 31. What is the nature of this realm that different orders of consciousness can exist there?

Its nature is the Dao. Nodes of Dao-consciousness have already been addressed in previous explanations in relation to human consciousness. A node in Dao may just as easily comprise a non-terrestrial disembodied conscious being. The fact that such a node can be mobile, and that it can possess individual will and identity, is a simple reflection of the identity comprising a node of the Dao.

Unfortunately, this is a circular argument. Nevertheless, it is the nature of the Dao to manifest nodes. It naturally enables a node to gain an accretion of various faculties and to occupy a realm of its choosing for a purpose also of its choosing. That is the sense in which an individual is cast from the Dao – and we identify at this moment that the term "cast from the Dao" is notionally expressed as the natural spontaneous development of a node of the same substance as the Dao.

Of course, the term substance is false, for the nature of the Dao is without substance, in a conventional sense. Yet, from the perspective to which we speak, which is that of an embodied mind manifesting bio-consciousness (which is inevitably the perspective adopted in almost all instances of immersion within the time-bound realm), it is appropriate to recognise that the idea of the phenomenon of a node of the Dao spontaneously self-assembling is a feature and construct of Dao-nature.

There are no limits to the extent to which this is possible. There are no limits to the theoretical magnitude of such self-assembly. There are no limits to the varieties of self-chosen purpose which such manifestations of Dao may determine for themselves. This applies just as much to the Dao-consciousness manifest in association with the individual embodied conscious being, identifiable as homo sapiens sapiens, as to any other species. Of course, there are normal ranges. Which implies that there are also abnormal ranges.

TERRESTRIAL EMBODIED CONSCIOUS BEINGS

Q 32. We human beings overwhelmingly assume that we are the only self-conscious beings on this planet. But the nature of consciousness appears to be more complex than this. For example, a group or hive mind is discernible in the activities of many creatures, such as flocks of birds and the organisation of ant nests. On the other hand, whales and dolphins have a brain comparable to the human brain, are highly sociable, and display the functions of language. And many people consider they communicate with their pets. So it appears that rather than thinking that human beings are the only self-consciousness beings on this planet, it might be more useful to think of consciousness on Earth as a series of discrete levels, each with its own characteristics. Your thoughts on this?

Given that human beings are not the only self-conscious beings on this planet, it is completely appropriate to imagine that there are a range of such loci, being nodes in Dao-consciousness. These have levels of organisation appropriate to the organism with which they are associated.

Given, additionally, that it would be inappropriate for an ant to be endowed with a human-level Dao-consciousness simply because of the ineffectuality of the processing functions within the ant brain, it would be inappropriate for the typical Dao-consciousness associated with an ant to be associated with a human organism and the information processing capacities of the human brain.

Therefore it is reasonable to conclude, and we affirm, that manifestations of Dao-consciousness occur in a range of orders of complexity and functions appropriate to the organism with which they are intended and with which they self-elect to associate.

Q 33. Where does the group or hive mind of flocks or nests reside? In the mind of the Earth? In the fourth dimension? At the third dimensional genetic level or at the quantum level? I ask because ant nests can exist for decades, maintaining the same social structure and functions, even though all the original ants have died long ago.

Group or hive minds, for instance of avian species or nests of social insects such as ants, reside in the same place as every other variety of Dao-consciousness. That is, they reside in the Dao, in the unmanifest, which is associated with, and interpenetrates, organisms existing in the physical domain. Given that the Earth has no mind, and that the meaning of the fourth dimension is unclear, it is sufficient to reiterate the distinctions already made, because it is not in the third dimension, nor at the quantum level, but, as we have said, on the level of the Dao. In this instance, group or hive minds may be expressed in terms of a level assigned to them on a notional axis in agapéic space.

Just as human beings have a range of occupancy on the agapéic space axis which is notionally from 25 to 35, and elementals have a range on that axis from 15 to 25, so we find it convenient to allocate those species that function with a group mind a position on that scale between 10 and 15. This is the purpose of the scale: to provide a linear representation of level and complexity in increasing orders of magnitude as assigned by the units on the agapéic frequency axis.

Of course, this is a metaphor. It is not the reality. We repeat that it is a convenient model by which to assign some numbers to the manifestation of the range of order of complexity and functionality associated with the different kinds and species of conscious beings.

Given that it is designed to incorporate everything from zero to the ultimate of manifested Dao-consciousness, the range on the agapéic frequency scale provides an aligned and progressive assignment, in numeric form, to diverse and complex reality. In that sense it is simplistic. But it has utility in that it facilitates understanding when discussing the diverse features of Dao-consciousness existing in association with bio-consciousness.

We have already spoken of the extent to which Dao-consciousness may be assigned a limited duration of existence. With regard to the existence of a node, from the perspective of Dao-consciousness – and this is the difficulty of speaking within a realm in which time prevails – there is a potential assigning of existence within Dao-consciousness, and there is a potential assigning of nonexistence. Yet duration has no meaning from that perspective. Therefore emergence is a more useful concept, except to the degree that it intrinsically contains time. Accordingly, the more fundamental notation, if one can think of it in such terms, is as simple existence

RANGE OF OCCUPANCY ON THE AGAPÉ SCALE

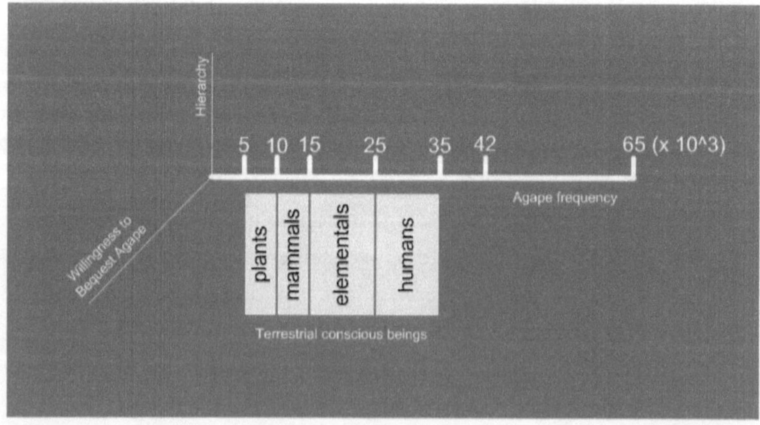

FIGURE 10.1

or nonexistence. One can imagine that a node exists and can associate with a biological organism for the duration of that organism's lifetime, whether it is an individual or a social cluster, and so think of the hive mind in that context.

Given that when a Dao-consciousness ceases to associate with a bio-consciousness the Dao-consciousness does not also cease to exist, a shift in perspective needs to be adopted when considering the contrast between bio-consciousness and Dao-consciousness.

An agile and alert mind can simultaneously represent both perspectives in its awareness, making it possible to understand the association of Dao-consciousness with a bio-consciousness, and also the non-association of Dao-consciousness with that bio-consciousness, which occurs when the bio-consciousness dies. The Dao-consciousness continues to exist, being unaffected by the death of the bio-consciousness. It may subsequently associate with another bio-consciousness, as a matter of the expression of its will. Given that such an association is in its own interest, when an opportunity is deemed appropriate, it will likely do so.

Thus we address the confusion regarding the death of the bio-consciousness – the absence after existence of the bio-consciousness – with the ongoing presence of the Dao-consciousness that elected to associate with that bio-consciousness for the duration of its lifetime. This is true no matter what the magnitude or complexity of bio-consciousness. It includes the group mind species being considered here.

Q 34. What is the situation in particular with whales and dolphins regarding their status as consciousness beings?

Given that whales and dolphins are consciousness beings in bio-consciousness terms, we can assert that they have been deemed appropriate and available beings for Dao-consciousness to associate with. The usual expression of that is in the language of ensoulment. So, yes, they are ensouled. Few other species are, and not usually to the degree that one would find that identifiable. And not for the duration of a life, as we have referred to elsewhere, but commonly only temporarily, for a particular purpose, and particularly a communicative purpose.

Q 35. What is the situation with dogs, given that they have been domesticated over thousands of years and have developed a rapport with human beings?

As with our response to Question 34, dogs are an expression of developed bio-consciousness. They are occasionally associated with higher levels of Dao-consciousness. That explains the unusual purposive behaviour some-times observed in that species. As we have stated, they have their own level on the agapé scale, and have an ongoing existence in Dao-consciousness.

When an individual has the capacity to move with freedom up and down the agapéic scale, such identities can be perceived, met and inter-acted with. Their characteristics may then be noted in terms of energy-signature. There are examples, available in accounts of Agapé School group meditations, of interactions between meditators and canines, in which mutual awareness occurred. However, such incidents are rare.

The mobility of those meditators enables them to contact and associate with beings on other levels of the agapéic scale. This is because they are predisposed to perceive the domain of Dao-consciousness, or at least the astral domain, to use traditional terminology. As a result of their movement up and down the agapéic scale they encounter different orders of beings who, through their own capacity for movement, have elected to come to the level occupied by those meditators, or to come part way towards them, and thereby attract their attention. This association on a similar level makes communication possible, temporary though it may be.

In the same way, this mobility has enabled some meditators to experi-ence rather different orders of being, that is, normally occupying ranges other than the human spectrum of 25–35. By that means they encounter species such as canines, elementals, and also higher orders of being whose task it has been to interact with them in order to convey this transmission of understanding.

Q 36. What is the consciousness of vegetation, particularly large trees?

There will be found on record two instances of association with trees. This represents a very far excursion from the domain of the human. The range of agapé frequency appropriate to the range of species identified by the English term plant, we nominate as between 5 and 10 on the agapé scale.

Q 37. Any comments on other species?

We have made attributions regarding the range occupied by a few species on the agapé frequency scale. We have identified them as being 5 to 10 for the variety of plants and the appropriate degree of Dao-consciousness manifest in such species, 10 to 15 for the general range of mammals, 15 to 25 for the range of elementals, with 25 to 35 being the typical range for human beings.

Above 35 we assert that we ourselves are situated at a location able to be assigned as 42 on that scale. Given that we decline, because we may not in this transmission assign orders of being other than that, and in particular higher than the level of 42, we will say no more. We now turn to terrestrial disembodied conscious beings.

TERRESTRIAL DISEMBODIED CONSCIOUS BEINGS

Q 38. Are disembodied beings living among us on Earth? If so, what are they and what is their relationship to human beings?

We have on many occasions facilitated temporary co-association between disembodied human beings and the cohort of meditators within many of the meditation groups forming the basis of this transmission of spiritual wisdom. Such examples can be found among their records, demonstrating that there are many disembodied human beings.

We can now be more specific by saying that they are the Dao-consciousness remnant, accumulated information record, personality characteristics, and memories associated with a deceased human body. In addition to such deceased human beings in their Dao-consciousness form, there are various conglomerations of such identities, clusters such as have been encountered and are on record.

All such clusters have not been encountered, for the specific reason that the most negatively biased clusters constitute a condition of danger to the ordinary loving and living human being. Part of the reason that they have not been encountered in our meditation groups is because they inhabit ranges within agapéic space which the human does not ordinarily occupy. To describe such ranges would require an extension to the simplified and simplistic model already given concerning agapéic space. We decline to do that,. What has been given is sufficient.

Q 39. We human beings assume that whatever form of consciousness animals possess dies with them. Is this correct? Or does the consciousness of animals continue after death?

We have already addressed the distinction between the bio-consciousness and the Dao-consciousness of animals. The Dao-consciousness continues, the bio-consciousness does not.

CHAPTER ELEVEN

On Human Embodiment

18 May

07:39. This morning is cold and clear with a moderate southwester. Whitecaps on the water are shining in the morning sun, the rays of which are yet to arrive here in the valley. It is thirteen degrees inside.

I received a call from P. yesterday about police visiting my house. Evidently, someone had given them my address as their home address. This has raised my hackles and caused a response of imagined conversations with them that has disrupted to my equanimity. I imagined a variety of scenarios, including a reaction strategy by dark powers against this transmission. But it is much more likely to be to give access to the aerial installer for my neighbour to receive SkyTV, or some such. I will sit for a while to get over it.

Such a long day of typing yesterday. I was glad to get into bed and slept well. I didn't walk yesterday, what with rain and typing. I hope to complete the last fifteen questions today. But they are deep and may well require extensive responses. And that is fine by me!

08:44. I had just finished my morning coffee and was reading through the last questions in the section on human embodiment. As soon as I finished reading them I got chilled and heard, "We will speak now." I was planning to sit for a while to centre, but it appears we're straight into it.

These deep questions are deserving of extensive responses. We will therefore take the whole day to progress through them in the designated sequence. Not that the designated sequence is necessarily optimal in terms of a coherent description. Nevertheless, the structure of the questions is sufficiently detailed to harmonise one with the other and to enable a considered, effective and complete response. Where that is not the case, we will extend on the questions as we believe appropriate, in accordance with the questions' implications.

Q 40. I am assuming that the purpose of human embodiment is to experience life in a physical body in order to grow as an identity. Reincarnation is a necessary aspect of embodiment because only as a consequence of repeated incarnations do we learn all there is to learn on the physical plane and in human culture. I am also aware that whales and dolphins offer another line of embodiment on this planet, but that spirits do not appear to change species for embodiment.

What is your definition of the purpose of us, as spiritual identities, undergoing human embodiment?

Of course, this is a question posed from the perspective of an embodied individual in the mid to late period in its particular incarnation, who is a product of an extensive education system, and whose reflective attitude has drawn on a variety of influential sources, by which we mean books, encountered by that individual, Keith Hill.

We would comment that as individuals go in their term of embodiment, the man Keith Hill has made good use of his time. To be curious and to engage in reflective discourse in the way he has done is one of the more profitable options for the consummation of a life. You will note that consummation can take several forms, with the sexual consummation of a marriage of course being another form of consummation which occupies the minds of many individuals. That this individual has not fallen for that invitation is to his benefit rather than his detriment. Nevertheless, the shaping of a particular life is precisely the consequence of decisions such as that made at one time or another during the life.

The embodiment of an individual spirit in physical form is usually the consequence of a favourable prediction, a calculation, of the probabilities for a match between the intentions of the node of Dao-consciousness and the opportunities it has while embodied to extricate itself from a variety of self-limitations perceived by it to be a barrier to its full flowering as an autonomous, independently mobile, well informed and mature individual product of emergence from the Dao. Such a perspective is natural while occupying the domain of pure Dao-consciousness. From that perspective, embodiment offers the opportunity to meet and interact with old friends, to engage in various forms of mischief and amusement, and to act out of serious purpose.

The creativity inherent in engaging in a physical life begins before the commencement of an individual's co-association and coalescence with the body of a human embryo. We will speak to the occupation of non-human embryos a little later. The co-association formed is the outcome of a set of opportunities being sensed, the opportunities being to enable an individual to develop a new sub-identity, that is, a new lifetime personality.

The set of opportunities involves an individual engaging with others with whom arrangements have been made to meet, to interact, and to work out karma together, or perhaps even to make karma together – although this last is not usually an objective. Embodiment in the physical domain also offers rich opportunities to meet and to associate with others of unlike kind.

For that is the principal opportunity: to meet others of radically different make-up, perceptions and attitudes, whether that meeting involves arrogance or self-grandeur, slimy obsequiousness, or even expressions of downright evil nature. The loving individual has no opportunity to interact with these characteristics in their ordinary location in Dao-consciousness. That is because Dao-consciousness is differentiated by level.

The level being referred to here is that of hierarchy. Hierarchy is earned. As we have stated previously, it is a product and sum of loving acts performed within the duration of existence of a node of Dao-consciousness.

Therefore individuals who are naive in their experiential development as a unit of Dao-consciousness may come into the realm of the human, to use just that example (and there are many others), and make decisions, but be ill-prepared to endure the consequences. Given that at such an early stage of their development they have little familiarity with the set of controls associated with occupying a human animal body, they are very likely to be over-ridden in their decisions by human animal biological impulses, and to be ineffective in their attempts to control the rampant set of human animal emotions.

Human emotions are the product of a very long period of competitive socialising with both peers and enemies, in the sense that over the eons humans have been prey for several other species. And so the normal mammalian emotional and biological reactions experienced during a life give rise, in many instances, to opportunities for provocation and response, such as avarice, power or anger, which consequently generate considerable karma. By this we refer to reactions which result in others being radically disempowered, confined or killed. Such reactions lead to a train of consequences that often include retribution at the level of individual, relative or clan. These chains of reactions subsequently generate potent conditions for engaging in further actions that are necessary to restore, then eliminate, karma and karmic indebtedness, especially in relation to an individual's record of experiences gained during an incarnation.

There is much to be learned as a product of all of this activity. We would point in particular to the generation of awareness of the contrast between, on the one hand, reactions involving anger, provocation, jealousy and all the strong human emotions, and on the other, those emanating from the intrinsic loving nature of a spiritual identity and of the Dao-consciousness that comprises it.

In many instances, the node of Dao-consciousness, commonly called the spirit of the associated individual, has been appalled at the outcome of what has been a naive wish to engage with the domain of humanity. As a result, the individual usually retires to reflect at length in order to discover and understand motives and to repair the consequences that accumulated in the course of that one human life experience.

We realise that what we are saying in describing the product of a naive node of Dao-consciousness in the early phases of its occupation and experience of the human life form has previously been described in many cultures. We neither intend nor provide any radical departure from those past descriptions, because they are not wrong. What we are saying diverges from them only in terms of minor differences in terminology.

So the distinction to be obtained by the individual, over the course of multiple incarnations within the human life form, is that there are parameters of control. There are means by which an individual progressively comes to understand the ways a life form may be modified, particularly which sets of reactions can be inhibited, in contrast to those which cannot.

Speaking of the typical experience of an embodied individual through their sequence of lives, the masterful Dao-consciousness node (if we may express it in that way in order to avoid contamination by traditional terminologies) thoroughly understands the characteristics of the body they have grown in association with. This is because they have influenced its development in specific ways throughout the term of its personality development. Furthermore, as a result of accumulated wisdom, the masterful node has also chosen sets of associates to mix with and other sets of associates to avoid. The knowledge that such a mature spiritual identity exhibits is reflected in the life experiences acquired during that incarnation, the aim being to influence its experience towards the positive and away from the gruelling.

What such a node actually does, of course, is to lift the horizon of its regard from the mundane, superficial and inconsequential into opportunities to benignly or constructively influence the society it inhabits. This facilitates breadth of perspective and depth of understanding, which in turn leads it to be regarded by its brethren as containing wisdom and maturity.

These are the opportunities created when the individual node engages in human embodiment. It is for the enrichment of the soul, to use that traditional terminology.

Q 41. Given the vastness of the universe, there are certainly many other planets available for spirits to utilise for embodiment. Why was the Earth selected for the embodiment experience? Is there some particular benefit offered by this planet?

From the perspective of an embodied individual such as has generated these questions, it is extremely difficult to imagine in any full and complete way the range of opportunities which are in fact available to a node of Dao-consciousness from which to select a range of opportunities in order to come to spiritual maturity. The sets of opportunities are very rich. What primarily draws spiritual identities back to this particular planet is to extinguish karmic debts with those with whom it has generated them.

There are many other opportunities. But we will not describe them. Suffice to say that this human animal species has a variety of opportunities, which are mostly mirrored in other species in other planetary and galactic systems, and that occasionally one of them is chosen for embodiment as an alternative to coming back to this particular planet.

There are many, many such galactic and planetary systems from which to choose. Some identities elect to specialise. Some do not. The sets of opportunities are sufficiently rich as to make this planet one of many. It is simple convenience as much as anything else which leads a node of Dao-consciousness to occupy itself in the generation and extinction of karma on this planet, as opposed to making use of any of the numerous other opportunities available.

In that sense, there is nothing special about this planet. It has a particular variety of environmental niches, it has a set of carbon-based life forms, and, in many instances, it has a relatively benign environment.

From the perspective of Question 41, there is an inevitable bias towards the expectation that a node of Dao-consciousness will occupy a land animal species such as the human rather than a member of its cousin species which occupy the watery environment. In fact, all of these are merely opportunities to undergo particular experiences. However, it is generally the case that a node will not switch species, because in many instances the parameter-sets differ rather wildly from one species to another, and acquiring the factors by which to control the organism of one species is so challenging that only particularly courageous individuals attempt to learn to control multiple species. That is sufficient reason for selecting one particular species of created life form to occupy and to disregard the rest.

In that sense, is there some particular benefit or challenge provided by this planet? No. It is not reasonable to expect that is the case. We have enumerated the benefits in part. Other than that, it is a simple choice by a consciousness node in the way that we have described.

Q 42. When did the process of embodiment on this planet begin?

The age at which the process of human embodiment on this planet first began was not long after the development of the human. And we speak of the human in terms of homo sapiens sapiens, because that is the implicit framework contained within the question.

The development of homo sapiens sapiens is relatively recent, but much older than the specified 200,000 years. We will leave it to the archeologists to define the time frames. We have no interest in making unsupportable statements that conflict with the current theories of archeological biology. So we will frame it in developmental terms rather than in terms related to the number of rotations of this particular planet as specified in the historical record of years.

The era when homo sapiens sapiens became suitable for occupancy was the point at which a sufficient breeding population was established to engender a level of confidence that it would continue to survive as a viable species. Naturally, that took a considerable period of time from its initial evolution and subsequent development into a distinct line of species.

When, after observation, the decision was made that homo sapiens sapiens was a suitable container, and that a parasitising ensoulment process would be able to continue into the foreseeable future – which at that stage, and from that level, comprised the order of ten million years – the process of ensoulment or embodiment began.

The precise prognosis was that the species would allow not only the development, through continued embodiment, of individual history and karma, but also for the resolution of karma. Accordingly, any particular individual node of Dao-consciousness could be confident that the opportunity for specialising in that particular species would be sufficient and adequate to its chosen task of coming to maturity and no longer requiring embodiment in an organic species. Acquiring the necessary experience, and resolving karma, would enable it to move to the next level of spiritual development, and therefore no longer need to re-occupy that chosen life form. So that was the prime decision, based on this projection regarding the viability of the species.

Other species were considered. Other species have been occupied. We will speak of that shortly. But at the moment we seek only to establish the perspective from which a decision was made concerning the prospect of a node's development through association with a particular organic species.

We have already given an approximate time range through which the human is currently in process. It is inappropriate to be dogmatic in any assertion about such things. It is sufficient to specify a range of utility such that nodes of Dao-consciousness can comfortably envelop themselves in the human in a manner that allows them to achieve their purposes.

Q 43. You have previously stated that disembodied spirits have been visiting this planet since before creatures moved out of the oceans and onto land. Could you expand in this statement?

Contained within the response to the previous question is a perspective requiring observation of the planet over an extensive time period. The range of that period is of no consequence.

Recall that the overarching scenario of an *observer* developing a cosmic experiment provides the true time domain of observation, because prior to the beginning of that experiment there was benign awareness and intention by a node of intellect and purpose. Therefore any specification of a time period of observation of this particular planet is essentially meaningless, apart from a specification that it has always been under observation from before its beginning. That observation will continue until after its extinction and absorption by the local star.

To assign a number related to the annual rotations of the planet is absurd. The perspective is much larger than that. It is very difficult for the ordinary human, whether embodied or not, to have full comprehension of that simple fact. This is the purview of this transmission.

We recognise the difficulty in coming to a true appreciation of these simple things. Yet that is a strand of our purpose in illuminating this small corner of creation with our intended discourse.

Q 44. Scientists currently consider that modern homo sapiens sapiens dates back to around 200,000 BCE. Do you agree with this dating?

We do not agree with the dating. It is based on partial evidence and is incorrect.

Q 45. Prior to 200,000 BCE, species that preceded the modern human existed, such as homo sapiens neanderthalensis, denisova hominins and homo floresiensis. They in turn were preceded by homo erectus and homo habilis. Were these earlier species also used for embodiment?

The assumption that bodies were ensouled before the specified 200,000 BCE date? It is certainly true that that was the case. What species did they use for embodiment? Several: homo sapiens sapiens, denisova hominins, homo floresiensis, homo sapiens neanderthalensis, and some others. But not homo erectus itself, nor homo habilis, as they existed before a sufficiently positive projection of the survival of the near-human species was developed.

Q 46. Were the great apes used for embodiment?

Yes, to some extent. The suitability of those species to provide opportunities for intellect and purpose to migrate and complete karmic cycles was trialled. But it was concluded that it was more appropriate to access a different time period, rather than that when the great apes were the primary occupants of the available environmental niches. It was foreseen that metabolic and intelligence adjustments could be made to that species in such a way as to generate a sub-species that offered more suitable opportunities.

Bearing in mind that adjustments have been made in terms of biological imperatives at the DNA level, it may be said that suitable species have been bred from the available stock. In that sense, it could be viewed that evolution has been directed and/or hastened. However, that is an invalid interpretation, because outside of time any time is accessible. Nevertheless, there was an intervention in order to increase the probability of a viable proto-human species, the outcome being to establish an inhabitable species suitable for co-association by nodes of Dao-consciousness.

It is from pure self interest that this has been done. The activity of deliberately intervening in what could be thought of as evolution has been purposely carried out, not only throughout this universe, but throughout the multiverse, that is, throughout all the individual universes subject to experimental investigation, so that multiple suitable environmental niches might be occupied by varieties of species.

There is nothing radical about what we are proposing. Certainly, there is nothing improper according to human morality. The activity of intervention is constructive within the terms of the intention by which the multiverse was created.

Q 47. Related to the issue of time line, in 1978 footprints were found at Laetoli in Tanzania by Mary Leakey which date to 3.6 million years ago and appear to be human. In addition, Michael Cremo has drawn attention to evidence found in mines that suggests human occupation dates back millions of years. Cremo's view is that this data questions whether the evolutionary line that became homo sapiens sapiens descended from the great apes, or whether it was an entirely separate line. What is your perspective on this? And on Cremo's anti-Darwinian position?

We have already remarked on the use made of the great ape evolutionary line, in which a series of specific interventions at the genetic level were carried out so as to obtain a richer set of opportunities for the spiritual purpose of Dao-consciousness. In those terms, we affirm that there is an evolutionary line extending backwards in time from homo sapiens sapiens to the great apes. We decline to specify its exact form. But it will be found eventually that there is a traceable history. And, indeed, this is already evident from the DNA record.

Cremo's position is that he declines to be awed by his predecessors and has sought a simple summation and synthesis of speculative record. His position has been seen by traditionalists as a novel and sometimes reprehensible invention. Nevertheless, he is closer than many others in arriving at a synthesis of history which accurately reflects the opportunities which have been made, and taken, in order to generate the preferred hypothesis. The hypothesis is that on this planet there came to be a species suitable for occupancy, that would enable co-association to occur, through the process of coalescence by originating identities, being nodes of Dao-consciousness, with an animal species suitable for exploration and exploitation.

In that sense, we support Cremo's position. We also note that historically his viewpoint will be seen as partial, but essentially accurate.

Q 48. You have stated that our consciousness is bi-located. That is, while incarnated in a body we have both a spiritual consciousness and a physical consciousness centred in the body's brain. This bi-located consciousness must have had a huge impact on the way that homo sapiens sapiens has evolved. Your comments?

Bear in mind the statements we have just made concerning the bi-location of awareness, and particularly the link between awareness generated by the human brain, that is bio-consciousness, and the awareness within the node of Dao-consciousness. Bi-located awareness is the means by which the node of Dao-consciousness may influence the bio-consciousness and to some degree affect its choice-making. So bi-located awareness facilitates a co-association of the higher mind with the lower mind.

We would comment at length on this matter, adding to what we have stated previously, because it is fruitful for individuals to become alert to the arrival of impressions from the higher mind into the lower mind, and hence to become confident regarding the way that decisions offered up to the higher mind by the lower mind are fostered in order to optimise the life experience, so it might conform with the life plan.

The lower mind generally knows nothing about the life plan until it enquires. The enquiry is of the higher mind. The lower mind's awareness of, and ongoing consultation with, the higher mind enables the lower mind to learn of the existence of a life plan, to understand that its life experience is most favourably shaped by acting in accordance with that life plan (with satisfaction or regret being felt at the end of a life depending on the extent to which the life goal was achieved), and to generate a constructive outcome for a particular life from the perspective of probable future life occupancy. Such consultation provides the optimal path for ensuring a life develops in a direction that reflects, and achieves results that accord with, the life plan.

In traditional religions, individuals who wish to understand their life plan are directed to pray. The activity of prayer is insufficient. What is also required is listening for the response, which may easily be missed. There is nothing wrong with prayer. It can play a valid part in the moment by moment invocation for guidance from the higher mind. What is equally required, however, is stillness. This creates a suitable environment in which the lower mind consciously observes the responses which are a natural product of the questioning process, whether the questioning be via prayer or by using any other technique.

The dialogue in process at this present moment is the product of a practised information exchange between the higher and lower minds. Each person, in the context of any given life, has the potential to develop an easy collocation of these two minds and establish an easy, fluid and rich communication between them. What is required is a technique for framing questions and seeking information, and effective techniques for the perception, assessment and interpretation of the responses given by the higher mind to the lower mind. These are the primary tools for achieving communication between these two locations in consciousness.

The contamination of such communication by the master-slave relationship promulgated in some religious traditions, or the spoiling and deconstruction of such information by an arrogantly independent human personality, often renders the inter-consciousness communication that we are describing essentially impossible. The problem is not the consciousness at the level of the higher mind. The problem is the character of the developed personality at the level of the lower mind.

In this context, there are techniques that optimally may be conditioned into individuals, either through socialisation within the family, by which a parent actively or passively models behaviours to their children, or through encouragement at the societal level, whether via education or via its absence. These may act together to produce individuals who have the option of pursuing life paths in which they profitably engage in the working out of karma.

There is a very important distinction to be made between the spiritual idealist position, whereby every individual life is structured towards its most productive result in terms of optimising communication between the higher and lower minds, and the competitive human idealist position, whereby no account at all is taken of human communicative possibilities, and instead full reign is given to the passionate human competitive nature.

Outcomes produced by this latter position include individuals seeking to survive or take power over others at any cost and being acquisitively alert to the best personal outcomes in social or financial terms. Of course, in less civilised conditions this outright arrogant human drive for dominance and survival is exactly what is required in order to be optimally competitive. And, naturally, all of these outcomes provide rich opportunities for nodes of Dao-consciousness to work out karmic patterns. However, we specifically deny competitive idealism is an optimal mode of behaviour and attitude to be adopted within the human population.

What embodiment makes available is a range of occupancy opportunities for evolving nodes of Dao-consciousness. There is nothing wrong with the fact that only a few places on this planet offer what could universally be agreed to be the most favourable conditions, according to higher mind principles, for establishing an idyllic lifestyle and developing what is optimally advantageous to humanity spiritually.

The determination provided by the steady-state model of spiritual development presupposes that any particular destination chosen by a node of Dao-consciousness involves a dynamic convergence that matches optimal karmic assignment with the opportunities offered by a given life. To facilitate this process it is necessary that there be a wide range of ongoing opportunities that stretch into the unforeseeable future, in other words, beyond what can be foreseen in any terms conceivable by the human mind. Naturally, this wide and dynamic range offers opportunities for the full array of human animal emotions as well as for refined spiritual emotions.

The two complementary idealisms of spiritual idealism and competitive humanity idealism are both required in perpetuity, at least within the ten million year time frame. Therefore nothing is wrong with human society at any level. Nothing is wrong with the identities that manifest in their diverse range as developed personalities within humanity. It all constitutes rich sets of opportunities for any node of Dao-consciousness to exploit – which they do, from the most sublime to the most horrific. In that sense, this transmission offers an amoral description.

It is completely appropriate that there are all levels of reaction to this perspective, because such reactions are precisely part of the opportunities available to each developed personality as it seeks to organise and align itself in order to optimise its life outcomes – whether those outcomes involve optimal education, optimal nutrition, optimal power, optimal money, optimal civic organisation, or optimal criminal organisation.

We recognise that there will be such a variety of reactions against these statements as to necessitate a benign resolve to ignore them. That is not inappropriate, as all is choice. The wide spectrum of opportunity has partly been created at the spiritual level so as to engage every possible set of reactions. With that we rest our case.

Q 49. You have previously stated that, as disembodied spirits, we are like parasites in the way that we use human bodies. Could you elaborate on this statement?

In a similar vein to our response to the last question, the term "parasite" has been provocatively used as a means of detaching any particular individual from their fond beliefs regarding the benign association between Dao-consciousness and bio-consciousness and the consequent development of a human personality. It is true that the association is benign. It is not true that it is necessarily supportive of the continued existence of that particular personality.

In that sense, the life cycle of a parasite in organic terms may be to sustain the life of its host, and many parasites do this. But other parasites eventually end the life of their hosts, and we think of the varroa mite on honey bees. Although it is counter-intuitive that the ending of a life by a parasite can ever be considered optimal, the validity of the process of making choices requires that some parasites do precisely that. It is no different with respect to the coalescence of a node of Dao-consciousness with an embryonic human, the intention of this coalescence being to achieve a fruitful outcome for that life. For a fruitful outcome may involve a premature death. We will give an example to support this point.

Suppose it is intended for a life to include an opportunity to redeem karma. Suppose that outcome optimally involves a group of isolated individuals struggling in a worst-case scenario, with death by starvation likely to occur before intervention by rescuers. And suppose that one individual in that group is desperately needed as food to enable the others to survive until help arrives. Such a situation has occurred on two or three occasions in relatively recent history, when an aircraft crashed or a ship was wrecked and the small number of survivors found themselves in desperate circumstances, without sufficient food, but knowing that if one was eaten then the others may survive.

It may then be that, as a consequence of conscious and deliberate willingness to dominate in order to survive, one survivor is involuntarily killed so the body may provide food. Or, alternatively, in loving and compassionate submission to the needs of the others, one may decide to voluntarily conclude the term of their life. And by that we include both the options of suicide and ritual slaughter.

Each of those situations may provide an opportunity for a particularly poignant karmic outcome. The desperate taking of a life, driven by the animal need for sustenance, is one scenario. And the voluntary gifting of a body no longer required, at a time when such a gift facilitates the survival of others, is an opportunity rich in connotations for love.

It is completely appropriate that even these desperate conditions exist. It is part of the spectrum of human association and experience. In that sense, the parasite on the human, that is, the node of Dao-consciousness, may use an opportunity to express its love for other co-embodied nodes and enable them to continue their association with their animal host by giving up its own association. From the perspective of the lower mind, that choice is almost incomprehensible. From the perspective of the higher mind it may be very simple. Given that such a scenario may very well be constructed by a set of individuals known to each other on the soul level, to use that language, then such a situation may offer the opportunity for potent karma to be resolved between those involved.

By means of this scenario we present an opportunity to consider a different perspective on embodiment and purpose. The giving of a life in contrast to taking of a life is one of the prime determinants of karma, which gives rise to indebtedness on the soul level. The compensation of the giving of a life is a radical act of love and usually elicits respect. It may also elicit many other emotions in the embodied human, hence its poignancy. We offer it as an opportunity to contextualise the viewpoint regarding parasitisation of the human.

And with that we will take a break.

CHAPTER TWELVE

On Coalescence

11:10. I'm perceiving what seems to be an illustration of the way in which the attention can be preferentially focused from the range of full attentiveness into the physical domain and then transferred through to full attentiveness to agapéic space. It's the transition from physical space to agapé space and back again, and it shows that partial dual attentiveness is possible in the sense that by retaining some awareness of both physical space and of agapéic space one can be alert to input from both domains. I also note that there is the possibility of a video rendition of this, achieved by the blending of superimposed sets of axes or coordinates which may effectively illustrate the effect of transition as attention is moved from one set of coordinates to the other. What a teaching tool it could be if formulated in those terms!

> And we would come to reinforce the presence of that phenomenon as a teaching tool, as a means by which to inculcate into those curious few who manifest the objective of dual simultaneous awareness for its optimal qualities of, one could construct it as being, the sum or the doubling of information-sets. We will return to this video project at another time. For now the necessary attention is a focus onto the finalisation of the questions from Keith Hill, numbers 50-52.
>
> There are errors of expectation in the construction of these questions which we will attempt to address in processing them one by one. And so on to coalescence.

Q 50. I next wish to ask about the way our spirit is embedded in a body to create an individual identity that is a mix of the animal and the spiritual. In Peter's book Guided Healing *you call this embedding coalescence, so I'll use that term.*

For coalescence to occur it seems the spirit needs to be embedded or "glued" into a body. One possible mechanism by which this occurs is via the energy nodes on the body that are identified by Eastern traditions, such as chakras. Is the spirit's connection to the body sustained by attaching itself via these energy nodes?

We question the premise of Question 50 in the sense that any "gluing" of the spirit into the body is required. We deny the necessity for any gluing process or mechanism, or any such result.

The co-association of the spiritual identity with the embryonic physical identity, even though the embryo scarcely contains any component of identity at the time a spiritual identity seeks to co-associate with it, is entirely one of choice. There are no particular levers to pull or constructed components to manipulate. There is only an intention to co-associate.

Bearing in mind that the relevant components of the physical construct are mostly space, and also bearing mind that the spiritual identity does not occupy space, the dimensions of association are not physical.

The blending-into phase, if one can use that concept, is an insertion of the point of attention. A unit or node of Dao-consciousness has only to focus its intention, then sustain that intention, for there to be effective coordination between the two constructs, if we can use that term. It is the emergence of spiritual intention into space-time, with which it intersects.

To return to the air-fog metaphor, in the same sense that two adjacent particles of fog can co-associate and merge, a process in which the ionic boundaries of one droplet blends into the ionic boundaries of the other droplet to form a slightly enlarged ionic boundary comprising both molecules, it may be envisaged that the "droplet" of organic matter merges with the "droplet" of spiritual matter so that their "molecules" intersperse one with the other.

This is all that is required. That is why it is called merging, co-association and coalescence. One coalesces into the other, whereby the vast amounts of space in the construct of one is slightly filled with the components of the vapour, as one could imagine it, with those invisible constituents of agapéic space coming to occupy physical space necessarily delimited by the boundaries of the physical form. Not that it is constrained into those boundaries, for the energetic form is larger than the physical form ever becomes.

Here we remind the reader of the model, experienced by this individual, of the spiritual identity comprising an essentially invisible sphere with a quite small kernel at its centre. Coalescence is modelled as the kernel becoming lodged into the energetic structure, that is, into the aura, of the physical form at the location of the hara dantian.

That kernel is not a physical form. It can merge into, and be associated with, the physical, dissolved into it in the same sense that in a chemical solution the ions or molecules of various substances co-associate in the same space. The solution becomes well mixed when the molecules are diffused and distributed in equal concentration.

In a similar manner, coalescence enables a spiritual body, if we can use that metaphor, to coexist in the same physical space as its biological construct. However, there is a non-uniform distribution of the "particles" of the spiritual structure, as shown in the model of kernel and globular form, as they coexist within and around the biological construct of the human body. Or of any other body, for that matter.

So it makes no sense to think binding is necessary, in the sense of locking into association elements of the physical body or of its energetic counterpart, the aura, with the node of Dao-consciousness. When there is an intention to merge, then merging occurs. When there is intention to dissociate, merging is terminated. There is complete freedom to come in and out of association between the two aspects of the combined identity.

In that sense it is not reasonable to suggest that the spirit's energetic connection with the body is sustained by attaching itself via the nodes of chakras or acupuncture points, being minor features of the chakra system. And for this we will need to digress into a more extended description of the construction, function and purpose of the chakra system.

Again utilising the air-fog model, there is a mode in which the structure of unmanifest Dao-consciousness, at least conceptually, can first be converted into manifest Dao-consciousness, and then converted into electro-spiritual substance. This is in contrast to electrophysical substance, which comprises the physical components of the alive body, including the particles and expressions of physical matter from which the body is composed, the body's chemical constituents, the body's gases, liquids and minerals, and ultimately the body's flesh and bones. And so we assert at this time that a means of rendering the physical structure into its appropriate form and diverse functions is to recognise the necessary interaction between what we term electrospiritual and the electrophysical.

The physicist David Bohm has named a subtle component of reality the implicate order. We identify Bohm's implicate order with the auric level. In the sense we are discussing here, the aura is a structure in the implicate order. It is necessarily associated with a grown physical structure of the flesh and bones, such as the human body. However, by implication, it is associated with any alive organism on this planet. This is because materiality necessarily has an associated component of implicate order, as that is the means by which physical structure and function is determined. And so it is the implicate order which fashions structured nature and its varied functions, in association with the DNA of the developed physical form.

We recognise that this will be contentious. We do not insist on its truthfulness. But it is a useful model to consider the relationship by which the electrospiritual functions as a guide and map for the developed structure of electrophysical substances, performing a blueprinting process via which physical structure comes into existence in order to fulfil its life cycle.

The implicate order is distributed throughout the physical realm by virtue of the *observer*'s intention to develop the experiment-sets by which this universe exists. Thus the implicate order comprises those elements of intention and is directly responsible, acting as a consequence of that guidance, for both the substructures of the physical universe and for the manifestation of components of environmental niches that are suitable for life.

It is too complex to describe in detail the function of that transference, or the arising of physicality. But we reiterate that the manifest physical universe is a product of the *observer*'s intention, and that the medium through which that intention is transferred is the electrospiritual component of existence. The "order" part of the phrase implicate order is a recognition of that structured intention. The "implicate" part of that phrase is a recognition of implication as both source and consequence of involvement. It is more fundamental to describe that component of existence as electrospiritual, in the sense that the intention assigned to it is an overlay or superposition of the intention to manifest.

And so in the context of this question about the spirit's energetic connection to the body, we assert that the presupposition from which the question arises is false.

Q 51. In order for characteristics developed in one lifetime to be carried through into subsequent incarnations it appears reasonable to think that there is an energetic component that contains these characteristics, and that this energetic component is carried by the spirit when it leaves one body and reincarnates in another. Your thoughts on how characteristics are carried from life to life?

Many aspects define not only a physical body but also a developed social identity. Great variance is possible in the development of both a physical body and a social identity, which occurs as a product of the co-association of a spiritual identity with a physical embryo. This variance of both physical form and social identity continues through the processes of ordinary growth to maturity. The willingness this individual shows to consider all of these aspects in nuanced radical form is very helpful to these discussions.

In light of our prior description concerning the process of coalescence, and how the electrospiritual component directs the structure of the electrophysical form, it may perhaps now be more easily appreciated that the desire of a node of Dao-consciousness to manifest a physical form containing features of consequence developed during a prior identity is a matter of intention. It can be applied very early during embryonic development.

There is a similarity in essential nature between Dao-consciousness and the electrospiritual. As a consequence the implicate order may be altered when intention is directed at it by a node of Dao-consciousness. This mutability of the implicate order provides the means by which specific characteristics, qualities, malformations, or whatever else is intended by Dao-consciousness, are imposed on the structure of the physical form. This is not to say that there are not genetic level implications, consequences, malformations and impositions. They are separate sources of form and ill-form, and one should not be confused with the other. Reality is this complex.

Therefore, if it is perceived that certain qualities may be initiated and sustained in the physical form so as to conveniently and purposefully direct a particular life plan to its fruitful outcome, then the node of Dao-consciousness may deliberately influence or even generate malformation in the embryo in order to optimise coalescence.

On the other hand, genetics may intervene, and an embryo may grow in the womb into a marginally viable or non-viable state. If an embryo develops in a way inappropriate to the life plan of the intending spiritual occupant of that body, then there can be a cancellation of the intention to co-associate with it and the embryo is left to its own outcome. That outcome may be birth in a condition of malformation and non-viability, or it may spontaneously be aborted, or it may be terminated by a deliberate act from the spiritual level, although that is rare. It can also simply be passed over and have no spirit designated to associate with it, whereon it quickly dies, either at birth or soon after. These outcomes are all possible.

An individual node's intention to feature characteristics drawn from experiences undergone during a prior incarnation is generally for a specific purpose. That purpose may be to feature physical or personality characteristics identifiably associated with a particular now dead body. Or it may be quite unrelated to either. There is that much flexibility in the process. So it is not possible to assign strictly determinant cause and effect, due to the multiplicity of causal relations in force here.

Q 52. Presumably it takes time for the spirit to coalesce with its new body, both when it is still an embryo and when it is born and becomes a developing infant. What is your view of this process?

The implications and presuppositions behind this question are that in order for effective personality and awareness to form in bio-consciousness there is necessarily input from Dao-consciousness. This is true. In order for a bio-consciousness to manifest an identity recognisable by parents and other observers, it needs to be sufficiently developed. That process takes two years.

Personality is very largely a product of body language and verbal capacity. The structure of the mind develops as a result of the formation of the brain. So brain development is a prerequisite for the formation of the local personality. The brain, for the first two years in particular, develops so rapidly in terms of making connections between synapses, that that process determines the characteristics of individuality in the local bio-consciousness, the lower mind. Where the brain is insufficiently developed, little personality is observable.

By about the age of two years the structure of the brain is sufficient to allow its functioning to develop an observable mind, through the outward display of verbal and nonverbal behaviours. Observation of these personality factors have led some to postulate that these verbal and nonverbal behaviours demonstrate the merging of Dao-consciousness and its higher mind with the emerging lower mind. It is a false association and a false attribution.

Typically, the Dao-consciousness is available for manifestation, but is not accessed. Instead, it is the biological development and brain function development that together manifest the behaviour that is viewed as characterising a personality. The Dao-consciousness associated and merged with an embryonic human being is usually sensed only obliquely and occasionally. This is because all attention, particularly the mother's, but equally that of any other observing individual, is fully focussed on the physical manifestation of this new life form. Detached alert introspective attentiveness to agapéic space is required to notice the spiritual identity co-associated with the new physical entity.

Only when that observational mode is adopted may the qualities of the individual co-associated with the physical form be evaluated. This is the basis of assessments of identity, assessments of personality, of spiritual nature, and of spiritual identity, by which a few people may notice who it is that is present with this new young human being.

CHAPTER THIRTEEN

Epilogue to the First Phase

That completes our discourse as stimulated by the questions we in turn stimulated into the mind of the individual Keith Hill. This will not be the last set of questions. These will not be our last responses. We look forward to further involvement with these two in order to facilitate their life plans, that being to bring afresh, from this remote corner of the inhabited world, into the English language, a consideration of issues concerning mind and conduct, and an exploration of the theoretical understanding of the purpose and function of the human species, in order to constructively influence others at the highest levels existing in the human world.

We have no doubt that in due course some notice will be given at such levels. However, we note it is not predetermined that that will be the case. It is a consequence of whatever quality may be perceived in this stream of interaction. Whether or not re-spiritualisation takes place within the human domain, as an effective antidote to the scientistic perspective, depends on the breadth of human faculty, reason, opportunity and function.

The growth of the scientistic perspective is a natural consequence of the rise of science and reason over emotion, confusion, imagined deity and politically promoted human fealty to such imagined deity.

We note that there are many good aspects to every religious system that has been proposed throughout human history. At times they have given rise to less than ideal consequences, to which we have alluded at different times via our ongoing discourses. But it is not our purpose to denigrate such things. Rather, we acknowledge them as the working out of particular strands of intentions and incentives, developed by embodied human beings to support mutual coexistence, such that some few individuals come to benefit and the general mass of humanity does not. As we have previously asserted, there is nothing wrong with this, because they reflect the emergence of complex human relationships, they provide complex opportunities for decision-making by individuals, and they give rise to opportunities to generate and resolve karma. Thus they provide opportunities to educate nodes of Dao-consciousness, as we are electing to refer to such things.

The descriptions offered of what, in traditional terms, has been identified as humanity's spiritual aspect, has been done explicitly to reveal the fundamental level at which humans and non-humans become opportunities for the enrichment of the information collected by the elevated levels of Dao-consciousness – and by non-humans we refer to animal species of every kind, all being manifestations of nodes of Dao-consciousness brought into association with various species, that sooner or later gain command of their environmental niches and sooner or later become self-conscious.

The unmanifest is universal and universally present. Manifest Dao-consciousness signifies that consciousness itself is universal and universally distributed. The particular segmentation of consciousness apparent in the arising of nodes of Dao-consciousness, including the developed intention they manifest, is also universal. It is precisely because such nodes of Dao-consciousness are associated with the organic human species that this discourse has been introduced into the world of the human.

We bless its presence, which means we assert its positive nature to direct and expand awareness of humanity's function and purpose.

Well, goodness me!

24 May
[The following communication was received and recorded by Peter during an evening group meditation session.]

We have the opportunity to offer a summary and codicil to the recent exercise in responding to the set of questions stimulated and prepared through the man Keith Hill. The content of those questions was deliberately chosen to echo the most profound of historical teachings concerning ultimate reality. We have taken the opportunity to express this teaching again in fresh terms in English, while retaining links to traditional terminology, enabling connections to be made between traditional teachings, predominantly of the country of India, but more widely than that, extending to different languages and to distant times.

It has been our strategy to do this so as to refresh understanding from the perspective of inhabitants of the English-speaking world on this small planet, without them needing to learn other languages. This is particularly appropriate given the global reach of that language. And so the plan was hatched. We invite all to examine the framework of understanding, along with the metaphors and models, that comprise this expansive transmission.

The opportunity to consult the past is always available. Yet the past grows dim with the passage of time. And changes in language cause much to be lost to present understanding. So no matter what treasures have been conveyed in earlier eras, they can be rendered null and void due to transitions within landscape and culture and through the simple passage of time.

So the outcome has been devised whereby individuals, undeveloped in their sensitivity to spiritual direction, may have available to them, internationally and without boundaries, a refreshed understanding of the nature and purpose of human life at its deepest levels. This transmission is not just cultural, nor is it merely from one sexual perspective or another, dependent upon one's expressed gender, but is given in universal terms so as to bring again into the world of form what has been forgotten.

It is intended that each young soul who comes to this realm, or to any other realm, that is detached from spiritual understanding, separated from memory of identity, and disconnected from knowledge of who one is at the core of identity, that such individuals have available to them, at their request and via our response, a readily accessible, refreshed and detailed description of their purpose for life.

We commend it to you. It is of our design.

That came from a long way away!

CHAPTER FOURTEEN

Preparations for Second Phase

[At this point a ten week break occurred because all the formulated questions had been answered. During this period I read through and edited Peter's transcriptions of the answers so far, then worked out the remaining questions.

At this stage I felt that a number of questions required further elucidation. So I began by clarifying some details regarding animals and the electrospiritual field. I then continued on to the topics I had previously mapped out, regarding evolution, human consciousness, ancient religions and reincarnation.

While formulating this final set of questions I became increasingly aware of a presence looking over my shoulder as I worked, nudging and even directing me. So in formulating the following questions I used two techniques. Some questions came directly from me, being focused on issues I had long wondered about. Others arrived after I emptied my mind and sat in silence, waiting for thoughts to arise. When they did, I ruminated on them until I understood their content, then shaped them into questions.

After receiving the final set of questions Peter returned to Matapaua on 20 August for what became the first of two final retreats.]

20 August

14.30. After driving through rain, I arrived at Matapaua to warm sunshine. I texted various friends to advise them of my location and of my intention to be on retreat for about ten days. I don't yet know whether I will return for the meditation night at my home on the 30th. But I will definitely return for the Theosophical Society's inaugural meditation evening on 2nd September.

I have probably bought too much food, but am imbibing wine to celebrate the retreat's beginning. I felt happy this morning to be embarking on another retreat. Then I discovered I forgot my electric blanket. Shock, horror! I might have to go to bed dressed to keep warm. A warm northerly had the house at

18C. But as this is a south-facing beach, it cooled off quickly after I arrived.

I have brought my bench grinder to sharpen the kitchen knives, so that task will occupy my first days here. I then discovered that mice had been partying in the pantry. I couldn't face the clean-up today, so will do that tomorrow. Clearly, food has to be kept inside stout plastic containers to resist them.

I have been enjoying some music from my Breathwork collection. It settles me into a peaceful preparedness for deep meditation. I have also brought Keith's remaining questions, which I've just re-read in preparation for receiving answers in the days to come.

21 August

05:37. I have been disturbed by a mouse overnight. The food cupboard is a mess. I'll vacuum the crap out of it when it is light and replace the dud bulb in the hall light so I can see better.

The stars are thick this morning due to the skies being clear, calm and cold. Apart from getting up to scare the mouse into silence I have slept well. This seat is hard and unforgiving on my gluteus maximi. Otherwise all is well. A morning sit is in order, I think.

06:48. I enjoyed a peaceful sit and felt visited by a couple of identities. But what is the mechanism by which the felt approach is perceived? If the higher self approaches, how does it do so? Is it not already present in the hara location? So why would one get any perception of approach? Is the proximity of the guiding self what is referred to in Egyptian images of the pharaoh with the supposed sun god on their head? Is it all metaphor for spiritual reality? What is the cause of the fine vibrations experienced during such an approach? And what is the cause of their cessation? Is it merely the coming into similar vibrational rate? If so, why are no beat frequencies reducing to zero manifest, as I have felt elsewhere?

10:57. Awoke and was called to meditation.

Coming as we do into your domain in order to accompany you on this final part of the one hundred questions segment of the discourse that we have now carried forward over many years, we wish to begin with some preliminary comments. In order to accompany you in the manner of your preference, we will outline our intentions for this time period.

First, the settling-in period has been swift on this occasion. In no small way, the imbibing of alcohol yesterday was responsible for this. Of much deeper influence, of course, is the degree to which you have sustained the practice of attending to this level, being attentive to inward signals and conditions, and clearly differentiating between factors of the ordinary life and factors within the extraordinary life – by which latter phrase we naturally refer to spiritual existence and understanding.

Though you may be firmly settled into an apparently secure understanding of the nature of the spiritual domain and its origins and tendencies, we only have to put before you some contrary story or model and that fragile certainty is lost. However, having no such intention, we merely point to each individual's dependence on consistency. Over the centuries there have been many inconsistent stories. We propose to offer an explanation for how this comes about.

Each individual is a product of its conditioning within the physical, emotional and mental domains. Furthermore, the models of reality offered by industrial or agrarian societies, within which individuals grow to maturity, have the most extraordinary impact on their understanding. In asserting this, we refer to the metaphors inculcated into individuals by those surrounding them, with each metaphor aimed at identifying and explaining an aspect of their existence as a human being participating, with other species, in life on the surface of this planet.

Metaphors with respect to social relations, passed on traditions of spiritual explanation, rudimentary drives that propel towards procreation – these fill the minds of every person, including this one, during the formative years of each incarnation. Such explanations have been conveyed using varying degrees of force. And prohibition against error, whether self-prescribed or family or religiously-derived, in fact has conveyed each of them into a multitude of errors.

There is nothing to be done about this except to focus the mind towards a deeper understanding of how one communication is acceptable and another is not, and to give reasons why certain aspects of any explanatory system are deemed unwelcome because they are contrary to what has already been received, or to encourage the perception of them as adulatory or required responses.

The single strength in this particular individual's conditioning is that his father was conditioned by his own mother to question society's truths and values to such an extent that he adopted the role, or self-description, of free thinker. Subsequently, this individual's father consciously and deliberately fostered in his own children an unwillingness to take information on face value.

The single strength of this individual's mother's conditioning was that she formed, within her own family, a sub-group who did not accept the validity claimed for the Christian faith. In doing so she was part of the camp within her large family who questioned the motives and beliefs of their other siblings and their ready acceptance of the spiritual explanations promoted within their family.

And so this individual's parents agreed with each other to leave the indoctrination of their children to the State, and acquiesced to the educational values promulgated within State schools. The reduction of religious influence, and especially the rejection of Christianity within those schools during the period of this individual's early life, was pivotal. As a result, he viewed the formal instruction in Christianity that he received during the first year of his intermediate school as essentially fallacious and opinionated, and held it in contempt. In all this the values he carried forward into this life as a result of his death in prior times were merely useful.

And so, without claiming that all is accurate, for it is not, or that it is the full truth, for it is not, the series of models this individual has accumulated and promulgated – accumulated by him and promulgated by us – is the best attempt available within the fragile belief systems existing in 2012, at the beginning of this century.

Given that essentially all information has been given in the context of the twenty-first century (this individual's prior life being a preparatory phase), it can legitimately be called a twenty-first century teaching. We recommend this phrase for its utility when communicating with others. It is accurate. And it establishes a foundation on which there may be some benefit granted to this teaching by those who encounter it. That is all.

22 August
07:16. I was up late, but now feel well rested. Heard no mouse overnight, so the terrifying towering monster it encountered has prevailed – perhaps. The other night I stamped on the floor and banged on the shelves, then saw a blur as it ran, moving too fast for me to focus on it. I'll wash the pantry shelves today, as

the hallway stinks of mouse urine. I thought of printing photos of the results of mouse partying and pinning them inside pantry doors to encourage other users to use plastic containers for all food. Clearly cardboard and plastic film are no barrier to a hungry and resourceful rodent. It even excavated a channel in the chipboard floor under the door so it could get its fat belly out more easily!

We come on this occasion to answer the questions developed by Keith Hill as a consequence of his review of the previous answers.

CHAPTER FIFTEEN

Six Clarifying Questions

Q 53. I begin with four questions regarding the nature of consciousness, and especially the consciousness of animals and insects in order to clarify the information given in Chapter Ten. The first is:

In your answers to Q 33 to 37 you stated that animals and insects possess a consciousness that is a node of Dao-consciousness. Are the nodes of animals and insects different from the nodes of human consciousness?

In principle, the nodes of consciousness are no different. The election by a node of Dao-consciousness to explore opportunities within the physical domain lead it sometimes to one species and sometimes to another. In this manner a comprehensive selection of experience is obtained. The criteria by which choice is exercised are not significant. By that we mean that the experiences available across varieties of species are different in degree and kind, and also differ in the opportunities they present to explore solitude or social life.

For example, the categories of consciousness by which an ant encounters another ant and interacts with it in the field of awareness contained within its social group, that is, within the colony, provides an opportunity to explore trust in the greater good. In this instance, trust consists of a willingness to act as an individual, yet behave in a cohesive manner in the interests of the colony's survival. This implies willingness to act fearlessly in the face of a predator, or cooperatively in order to carry out other tasks.

The activities of the colony are such as to engage the attention and the loyalty of each individual ant. The particle of consciousness in an ant mind is subservient in its nature. Hence subservience as a protocol for living comes to be thoroughly understood, in terms of deference and work, as well as in other activities. The focus required to participate in an ant colony is continuous, with little distraction. So the ant's modes of awareness, although confined in comparison to the range of human modes of awareness, are sufficient that it is able to explore some categories of social life.

Q 54. What is the process of the emanation of animal and insect Dao-consciousness from Dao? Is it the same as the process that emanates human beings, or is it different?

The arising of a node of Dao-consciousness is a spontaneous event triggered by a local accretion in density. We referred on the last retreat to the tides occurring in the unmanifest leading to very long-term periodicity in emanation from the unmanifest to the manifest, and to tidal processes of very long-term periodicity in the manifested domain.

A similar and related process leads to the spontaneous emergence of Dao-consciousness. The metaphor applicable in this instance is that of the watery sea spontaneously emitting droplets from wave tips as a result of turbulent conditions. This is a perfectly adequate metaphor, as the chaotic conditions in that sea generate forces sufficient to fragment the sea.

And so, without specifying any more deeply than this, for that metaphor is sufficient, there come into being a variety of droplets, that is, spontaneously manifested droplets of Dao-consciousness, which consist of various magnitudes, if we may express it in that term. The natural distribution and magnitude of these droplets is relevant to their association with a variety of opportunities to experience bio-consciousness. For, within these unspecified and unspecifiable dimensions, a match is found between the magnitude of the node of Dao-consciousness and the opportunity to experience bio-consciousness, those opportunities having been seeded into domains distributed across the variety of life-forms existing in the array of universes.

The Dao-consciousness has unmitigated free will. Distributed bio-consciousness, comprising ecological niches and their organisms, constitutes prepared opportunities for a matching process to occur. So from the perspective of any given node of Dao-consciousness, whatever its magnitude, a spectrum of opportunity from which it may choose is available to it. There is not necessarily a large overlap between the opportunity-sets comprising one species and another. Nevertheless, there is some overlap.

Extraordinary individuals, by which we mean bio-consciousness identities, are sometimes distinguishable from their peers as a consequence of co-association with a node of Dao-consciousness of magnitude either extraordinarily large or extraordinarily small.

In every population there is the norm within the population and the outlier, to use that statistical term, whereby the individual bio-consciousness excels in its maximum or minimal capacity, if we can express it in such a way. And so is forged, through that range of co-association with a given species, the spectrum of competence observable in a population of mature individuals of any species.

That this implies a controlling input from the level of Dao-consciousness is no error. Each reader of this material will have encountered, during the course of their life, individuals who are either extraordinarily gifted or extraordinarily incapable of functioning as a human being, with little apparent difference in bodily level development or competence.

It is more complex than this, of course. We have already addressed the degree to which variation in experience, from the naive node of Dao-consciousness to the experienced node of Dao-consciousness, is reflected in individuals' capacity to function in human roles. So this is a second layer of definition, or determination, of competence. It applies to all species, insects and animals included.

Q 55. Does the Dao-consciousness of insects and animals live one existence or many? And what happens to their node of consciousness when their body dies?

Of course they live many. There is no necessity to limit the modality of existence of a species, or to assume it is different from the modality of existence of any other species. What is being discussed is the nature of the node of Dao-consciousness, which is true and valid across all species. The species merely serve as containers for co-association, providing opportunities for experiential learning, and no more.

The release back into non-association is common across all species. It is not a characteristic of the node of Dao-consciousness, which varies across species, but of the species with which is co-associated. This implies commonality of function across all species.

Q 56. You stated in response to Q 50: "Coalescence is modelled here as the kernel that becomes lodged into the energetic structure, that is, into the aura of the physical form at the location of the dantian." What dantian do you refer to?

In Chinese, Japanese and Taoist philosophies there are three primary dantians: the hara or navel centre; the heart centre, associated with the thymus gland; and the forehead centre, between the eyebrows, associated with the pituitary gland.

We refer to the hara-level dantian, not to the other dantians described in this question.

Elsewhere we have discussed our intent to refrain from fragmenting this teaching too much. Part of the reason for this is so it may be anchored into contemporary experience by a sufficient number of individuals who report their experiences. Among the human population as a whole there is a progressive narrowing of first-hand experience brought into general awareness. Among the various dantian, the hara-level dantian is the most commonly experienced, because it is the most able to be experienced.

The description of the higher-level dantians has been the preserve of exponentially fewer individuals throughout history. So if there was one individual who reached the extraordinary degree of sensitivity required to consciously function from the pineal-related dantian, there would be ten to one hundred individuals who function from the heart-centred dantian but would never reach that higher level. Similarly, if one individual reached the degree of sensitivity required to consciously function from the heart-centre dantian associated with the thymus gland, there would be ten to one hundred who function from the hara-related dantian but would never perceive the thymus-level dantian in a given lifetime.

That is because in round numbers, there is a thousand-fold lesser sensitivity required of individuals between sensing the lower dantian and that required to perceive the higher dantian. We do not deny the reality of the higher-level dantian. We nevertheless choose not to describe them in this contemporary teaching.

[Note: The range being pointed to here is 10 X 10 = 100 to 100 X 100 = 10,000 individuals. So if a person who can sense the lower dantian is, let us say, 1 in 100 in a given population, then one who can sense the pineal dantian is at least 100 times less common, and maybe 10,000 times less common.]

Q 57. Which of these various dantian do you see as the primary dantian where the spiritual kernel becomes lodged into the aura's energetic structure?

There is no primary dantian. All function. But not all are able to be perceived by any given individual. Most individuals have zero perception of their hara-level dantian. Sensitivity is the preserve of the sensitised individual.

However, what they choose to make of such finely discriminated input is subject to validation by others, creating a context of validity within which such input may be acknowledged and acted from. Those far fewer individuals who, in terms of their manifestation within the human form, act from the higher level dantian are correspondingly privileged, and comprise the wisest of individuals. [Note: The term "dantian" is used here to indicate both the singular and plural case.]

Q 58. This question is drawn from a recent newspaper report. Scientists recently discovered that in 1988 there was an abrupt jump in the amount of carbon dioxide being absorbed by soil and plants. The shift went from 3% to 10% of all carbon emissions being absorbed. Scientists were surprised because they had not expected it, and are currently unable to explain why it occurred.

What was responsible for this shift? Was it due to a feedback loop in the biosphere kicking in? Or to consciously initiated intervention on the spiritual level?

The capacity of the organic and inorganic world to absorb generated carbon dioxide, CO_2, is subject to a series of levels of absorbancy, in which increments in temperature initiate a geometric increase in absorption. Of course, the biggest single factor is absorption by the world's water.

Consequently, surface absorption by water, and absorption within the body of vast volumes of organic matter, comprise a dynamic equilibrium within an as yet unsaturated potential, such that as the planet warms so the capacity to absorb CO_2 gas is magnified. This is merely one mechanism of self-regulation built into the structure of the natural world.

In addition to this, we could claim there was spiritual intervention in order to sustain the population of organic species resident on the planet. But that would be both a false claim and an unverifiable one. The feedback mechanisms inherent within the planet's biosphere are sufficient to account for the self-regulating processes.

CHAPTER SIXTEEN

On the Electrospiritual Field and the Aura

*Q 59. In answering Q 50 you introduced the terms of electrospiritual and implicate order. As I understand your explanation, the *observer*, through its intention, has generated an electrospiritual field. Embedded within this electrospiritual field is an implicate order. It is via the implicate order that the *observer*'s intention to generate the experiment that is the physical universe is translated into reality. So, in a sense, the electrospiritual field and its embedded implicate order provides the medium via which spiritual intent is realised in the physical realm.*

*Accordingly, your explanation presents three levels: the Dao, which is also the *observer*; the electrospiritual field, which contains an implicate order; and the electrophysical field, which constitutes the entirety of the physical realm, extending from the sub-atomic zero-point field to the cosmic.*

Is this a correct understanding?

This is an adequate summary of what we intended to extend understanding across the various domains of unmanifest and manifest existence.

Q 60. Does this mean that when spiritual beings work creatively to adjust environmental niches, such as is achieved by elementals, or when the DNA of biological species is adjusted in order to make them more suitable for co-association with spiritual nodes, the work is done at the level of the implicate order rather than by directly manipulating physical reality?

In almost every case this is true. The exception is a memorable event commonly described by the term miracle. The frequency of miracles is very small, but not zero, which is why it has a special place in the terminology of religious history.

Q 61. You stated that the aura is an energetic structure that is associated with a particular physical body, but that it exists within the implicate order. I'm not entirely clear what you mean. What is your definition of the aura?

Our definition of the aura has already been given in a number of places. But we will reiterate. The aura is derived from the stuff of Dao-consciousness. By that we mean the implicate order is generated by Dao-consciousness in unmanifest form. In asserting this, we point to the original nature of the unmanifest and to the derivative nature of the implicate order. In tandem with the implicate order, a patterning intention is generated that enables the electrophysical to be organised into the functioning body of an item of bio-consciousness. The aura's patterning function is what facilitates this organisation of the physical. It is the means by which the plastic cellular structures of the physical body, being undifferentiated cells, are modified and imprinted with their particular and durable functions.

In that sense, a component of cellular structure is generated, then given its specific function and intended location. These provide the myriad important structural and functional components from which the physical organic body is assembled. This may be contentious. But we claim it is valid and true.

The aura is generated from the implicate order. It is a dynamic generation that performs an organising function for the construction and maintenance of any body, and in this instance we mean any organic body suitable for life. At the end of a body's lifetime, when the requirement for the maintenance of that physical organism ceases, the aura returns to that from which it came, that being the unmanifest.

This implies that every item of organic life has an aura, which is true. It also implies that the dissolution of the holon, to use Wilber's term, is a natural consequence at the cessation of the life of every organism, for it is the organising function.

Q 62. (a) What is the "stuff" of the aura? Is it electrospiritual or electrophysical? (b) Is the aura a function of the body or of the implicate order? (c) Does the aura die when the physical body dies? (d) What is the aura's purpose?

(a) The "stuff" of the aura is essentially electrospiritual. It manifests the electrophysical into a particular and relevant pattern. (b) The aura is a function of the implicate order and is a pre-determinant of the body. (c) It is possible to express that by saying that when the physical body dies the aura dies with it – although the term "dissolves" is perhaps more appropriate here. (d) In Question 61 we gave the response that the function of the aura is to organise physical, that is electrophysical, matter into specific patterns in order to achieve particular structures and functions. That is the purpose of the aura.

Q 63. In Guided Healing *you indicate how, during spiritual healing, energy is passed into the healer from the spiritual domain via the healer's aura, and that the energy is passed on via the receiver's aura. You also stated earlier that thoughts are passed from the spiritual domain to embodied nodes via the aura, not by using telepathy. What other functions does the aura have?*

Reference is made in this question to the communicative function implicit within the aura. This is a function of the patterning process of the aura and of the interaction between the electrospiritual and the electrophysical, in the sense that the aura provides a communicative link between the realm of the node of Dao-consciousness and the developed bio-consciousness. The phenomenon of resonance between these two modes of existence enables patterned communicative action to occur.

This patterning procedure is somewhat equivalent to the way that a high frequency electromagnetic impulse, or a continuous radiated frequency, can be encoded with lower frequency information as a means by which to disperse that information through physical space. Another analogy is the way that information is encoded into patterns of energy using amplitude modulation, frequency modulation or phase modulation, then distributed either via a wire, through a fibre-optic glass cable, or by using any other information distribution medium.

These various means of encoding and dispersing information are analogous to the patterns of information that are propagated by a node of Dao-consciousness, that is, by the individuality and its higher mind, into the lower mind of, in this instance, a carbon-based organism.

Part of the additional function of the aura is to enable the intellect of a node of Dao-consciousness to fulfil its potential to communicate. That this function is seldom identified as a valuable conduit for information is a feature of physical life, not of spiritual existence. That it is rarely regarded, sought after, listened to, and actually acted on, does not diminish its value. This function of the aura is also why it has been identified historically as the mode for communicating with the gods. In contemporary language, it facilitates communication with the higher self.

Q 64. How does an individual node carry away the information it has gathered during its lifetime when the body it has been inhabiting dies? Presumably that information has to exist at the electrospiritual level in order to be carried away.

(a) If this is the case, how does this happen?

(b) When the node is born into a new body, how is the information selected to have an impact in this new life transferred into it? Via the implicate order?

(c) Does the aura have any role to play in this information transfer?

Coming, as we do, from a distant realm in order to respond to these questions, we are confronted by the difficulties in communication that arise from the contrast between these modes of being. It is a complete myth that the mode of being at the level of the higher self is in any fundamentally and distinct way separate from, and foreign to, the way of being of the lower mind associated with the human body. We will speak specifically in relation to these two different levels of experience.

Of course, the mode of being within the higher mind is disembodied, and therefore has no organism or structure such as a physical brain to manifest thoughts, beliefs, attitudes and opinions. Instead, these things manifest within patterns of energy. We need to be more explicit about this process in order to provide a working model of the higher mind and to convey some idea of its complexity and adequacy for the task assigned to it.

Accordingly, imagine a ball, say a soccer ball, with the hexagons and pentagons forming a net around its surface. Now imagine every intersection on that ball connected radially both inwards and outwards, such that it forms a foam-like or cellular structure of interconnecting filaments. The density of the interconnecting filaments provides the means by which encoded information may be carried by the structural bonds forming the interconnections between vertices in that foam-like or cellular structure.

This is a visual metaphor for the patterns in agapéic space dedicated to transporting information into a globular accumulation. It is a suitable metaphor by which, from the perspective of this particular body with its organic brain and associated mind, an individual higher mind may be conceived and these things contemplated, invisible as they are. Or, at least, normally invisible.

The higher self structure is not fixed in any particular place, but tends to assume a level according to its attributes on what we may grossly term a level of agapéic frequency, given this level exists as a function of its position in relation to the axes of agapéic frequency, hierarchy and willingness to bequest agapé. Because most individuals are at similar, but slightly different, values on those axes, information is encoded in a clustered globular distribution through agapéic space, if one may think of it that way.

When the higher self despatches an aspect of itself into the realm of the human, it retains knowledge of its circumstances, emotions, perils, fears and acquired tendencies by virtue of the communicating link which has been described previously. That link is not physical. It is on the haric level, to use that terminology. It connects the higher mind to the hara level within the organic body's formational system, the aura.

When the body dies and is incinerated or decays, the formational structure of the aura dissolves. In the process of dissolving all the information contained within it is uploaded, to use that modern concept, as patterns of information conveyed through the connecting link.

One could imagine a metaphor of the spider's web applying here, with the node of Dao-consciousness despatching into physicality first one, then two, and eventually the thousand or so fragments of its being, each accumulating information and subsequently uploading it at each developed personality's death to create the corresponding higher self associated with that fragment.

This metaphor is sufficient. A great deal more detail would need to be conveyed of the nature of the exchange of energy involving agapéic space, the implicate order and the electrospiritual, for the detail to be understood. In the absence of that detail in this simplified model-set, we deem the metaphor adequate.

CHAPTER SEVENTEEN

Interlude: Four

24 August

06:36. I woke feeling rested after dreaming I was in my red sports car. It had a mind of its own and was ready, willing and able to move independently of my command. I wondered if it was possessed and had to stop to reassert control. But it seemed very powerful and I had trouble steering it correctly. Is that my strong self?

> Yes. You have spent many years taming the beast within. Now you can do it so well you are in danger of being mistaken for being dead. As in the dream where you wondered that if you meditated to dispossess the car while in it whether you would be interrupted by concerned passers-by!

Last night the climb up the steep steps towards Tapu Point taxed my knee tendons, but I continued climbing to the top regardless. I reviewed the instructions from the April retreat, which said to walk every day. Clearly, my body needs that stress or it will get even weaker. I am *much* too young for that! More to the point, I have much to do to fulfil my life purpose here and a fit young (or even old) body is essential for achieving that. Have I been depressed? Hell, yes!

15:00. I have returned from Whitianga where I bought an electric blanket on special, and found food containers, CFL lamps and USB extender and a 32GB USB memory stick. I stopped at Kuaotunu on the way back for an extended coffee break, then drove back here through more rain. This seems not to be a day for channelling.

As I nailed wooden moulding to seal the base of the pantry doors the mouse came back, checking out the interloper in the kitchen. I chased it. Then I felt compassion for its exclusion from the pantry and considered giving it cheese!

The white-faced heron has also been back, slowly pacing the lawn and eating insects with almost every step. Its gait held its head motionless while it advanced, its neck flexing perfectly to match its body motion. I held myself motionless until it was out of sight.

25 August

The poxy mouse ate the All-Bran that I left on the bench! And the rice! Clearly, nothing is safe from its ravages. I should love it. But I don't.

11:45. I have finished cleaning up the mouse debris, vacuumed the house, and washed and returned everything to the pantry. For lunch I boiled packaged tomato soup. Only eighteen years past its use-by date. I assume I'll survive.

26 August

08:57. I've again reached the point where I feel completely incapable of responding from within my ordinary mind to the questions Keith has generated. I've sat in meditation this morning, or at least attempted to do so, and felt a slow quietening. The excitement associated with the mouse and its havoc, the clean-up and repairs and modifications to discourage it and other rodents from invading this house, along with all of the other things which have occupied me in recent days, have meant that very little progress has been made in attending to the reason for which I have come to this remote place.

It may be that it is simply necessary to get to the point of conscious inadequacy within the lower mind to enable the influence of the higher mind to penetrate at the conscious level.

To which we would say the following. There has to be a relaxation into inadequacy. In other traditions, phrases such as the conscious "prostration before the Lord" and the "letting go and letting God" have similar meaning. They express recognition that the limited intelligence, competence, willingness, capacity even, of the lower mind, full as it is of arrogance and assertions of sovereignty, needs to be confronted without creating affront to it. It is from a posture of emotional and intellectual openness that the assault from the higher mind can begin – and in this instance we mean assault in the kindest way.

The image of a gentle tidal wave of compassion and love, spreading to all corners of known existence, including the territory of the lower mind, is what we refer to here. Slowly engulfing loving compassion can fully compensate for the lower mind's inadequacies, arrogance, foetid blindness and insolence. In tenderness towards all these expressions of incompetence, we simply say that we love them all. And that of feeling inadequate to the task, whatever the task may be, facilitates the introduction of the spirit's strength.

We have spoken in recent days that it is necessary to invoke the strong self. That comment was naturally interpreted as relating to the personality and aspects of its sub-personality. It is true that the subjugation of the strong self, and in this instance we are referring to the arrogant self-assertive sub-personality, is naturally identified by that phrase. Yet what we actually mean by the term "strong self" is the conjunction of the lower and the higher minds into one functioning identity, whereby the composite strands may unify and function in a condition of sufficient maturity and goodwill that any task may be accomplished.

It is from the condition of perceived weakness, (whether the perception be of indoctrinated weakness, feared weakness, submissive weakness, or seeing submissiveness as weakness), that we may rebuild identity utilising strong components to support those weaknesses. Because they are not just perceptions. There is some reality behind the perceptions. Hence shame and submissiveness must be fully confronted in order to learn and become confident regarding where true strength comes from.

No ego wants to know this. Every ego wishes to promote itself as adequate, competent and successful and to deny inadequacy, incompetence and failure. That is the point of acknowledging incompetence, inadequacy and lack of success. And that is why this one finds it troubling, for it is not his ordinary daily experience.

We invoke this as a true and continuous partnership, which provides a basis for the strength and determination required to continue. It is the foundation on which the enterprise of conveying this transmission into the world can successfully proceed. This partnership is a permanent feature now. None from any quarter may gainsay that.

It's strange, I get a sense of some leftward input saying, "Oh, bugger, that one got away!" It is accompanied by a sense that level is inviolable and inaccessible from that leftward input. That insight might prove very helpful.

11:26. I had coffee and cake, then walked to the top of the hill. After the invocation earlier, as I sat with coffee I felt unaccustomed joy at the beauty of the sea, sky, bird life, grass, moss and lichen around me, and delight at the sensory input of fragrances, sounds and the joy of being immersed in life. I caught the thought, "This is what I came for!"

How strange, unusual and pleasant not to be caught in thought and planning the next moment, but to happily be in this moment. Any concern or urgency to complete this seems distant now. The day is beautiful, sunny and calm with a flat blue sea. I think I'm alone again here.

I felt internally encouraged to sleep and received a comment that "an adjustment is required." I lay on my belly and had an image of someone focussing on the back of my spinal column. Brain stem? Odd.

16:18. I have walked the beach. The tide was out, exposing a few rock pools containing a population of hermit crabs. It was a fine clear day with not much wind so both the environment and myself were calm.

While idly watching the hermit crabs go about their lives, crawling here and there in the pool, I observed one, much bigger than the others, aggressively approach a smaller crab, about one fifth its size. By now I felt as if the atmosphere around me was particularly quiet and that I was included in these small lives, to the extent that I seemed to empathetically sense the emotions of the two crabs with astonishing clarity.

On observing the approach of the much larger crab, which was rapidly bearing down on it, the smaller crab reacted with a feeling along the lines of – and I here use words from my own vocabulary – "Holy crap! Hide!" It immediately reacted by retreating into the safety of its shell.

Apparently observing this reaction, the larger crab turned away and pursued its own interests, approaching another area of the rock pool.

The smaller crab peeked out and saw the retreating back of the larger crab. It then emerged from its shell, crawled close behind the larger crab, but without touching it, and adopted the swaggering emotional stance of: "I'm not scared of you! I'll take you on anytime!"

If there had not been the particular clarity around me at that time, I would find it easy to discount my perceptions of the interaction I observed between the crabs and attribute it to mere anthropomorphic projection on my part. But given Keith's question as to whether crustacea are be included among the animals that should be regarded as co-associates of nodes of Dao-consciousness, I can only point to my just described perceptions and respond, presumably. Although I did not expect it to be so. I guess if a social species such as ants are included, then it is reasonable to include crustacea.

We come to confirm the relevance and significance of the issue addressed while capturing the vignette of hermit crabs at Matapaua.

However, of greater significance is the question of the representation of crustacea. Along with fish, crustacea usually live a life of absorption within a dark, cold, and often muddy environment. That human beings tend to consider that environment to be uncomfortable, foreign, obscure and lesser is a simple consequence of the fact that they occupy a land-based realm where all species are seen with considerably greater clarity.

Of course, a predator's approach, whether seen or unseen, and whether of the same species or another, has the same potential outcome in both environments, which is for the prey to be eaten and to provide nutrition progressively up the food chain. But because most humans consider they possess superior status due to being the top predator, they are vulnerable to misinterpreting their "life at the top" as the only life there is.

In fact, most adult humans have largely forgotten the simple yet intense feelings of fight and flight. Moreover, when they do become aware of them they have no desire to physically engage with them, to whatever extent is required in order to ensure their survival. In that, they are more privileged than they know. Because it is normal for every other species to have daily interactions that generate intense feelings involving either surviving or submitting to dying.

That being the case, humans easily achieve an intellectual detachment from emotion. Such detachment allows us to discuss these things with a representative of that species, a discussion that otherwise would not be possible. Calmness is required as a predisposing factor to facilitate communication between the node of Dao-consciousness and its sub-component, the individual human mind. On the other hand, where the node of Dao-consciousness is co-associated with a species not capable of, and therefore not accustomed to, that degree of intellectual detachment, communication is essentially rendered impossible. In that case the role of the node of Dao-consciousness is confined to information accumulation rather than to communication.

To that extent, species that are consciously co-associated, that is, are aware of the relationship between Dao-consciousness and biological mind, and who joyfully participate in that relationship, remain a precious phenomenon. The subtle pleasure associated with the resulting communicative function is a valued component of our path with you. That is all.

I was very persistently cold at the beginning of that. Warming up rapidly now. I only want to sleep again. Any chance of channelling seems to be out the window. I got the comment: "We are making you tired."

27 August

Sat for nearly an hour. I saw an internal cavernous rectangular dungeon and perceived an oily black drip fall out of sight into the empty depths below. I felt it had been recently drained of its contents. I feel differently.

I heard: "Come another week to address the remainder of the questions." So I may go home today or tomorrow. But: "Tomorrow would be better." It would appear that a time of settling and integrating a different internal condition is required.

11:40. I slept all morning. I feel zero motivation to do anything. I think that eating a substantial meal then sleeping was the obligatory response, so I'm functioning on that very simple level.

I feel disconnected from my years of motivated striving towards completing my life task. Perhaps because the end is here? What are the real consequences of union with the higher self? If that is what has happened? What is true partnership? What is continuous partnership? How will it change my life?

We will answer the questions just asked concerning the nature of true and continuous partnership between the higher self and lower mind, and the changes in living that flow from that.

True partnership is union. This is explicitly implied by that statement. It does not imply a particular presence or absence of collocation of the higher self with the lower mind, because the capacity for the higher self to depart is retained. We mean, in this instance, that the spirit-sphere, to use that terminology, retains freedom of movement and is not locked into identity of location with the physical form. Rather, the higher mind's higher attention, if one may express it that way, remains intimately associated with the lower mind, but in a directing role, instead of the lower mind retaining its arrogant egotistic self-direction.

That continuous association brings a moderating influence to the lower mind, in terms of the consequences of having an internal directing function effective from that higher level, rather than from the passionate mind filled with motivations derived from the animal brain, the limbic system and the brain stem. That was the reason for the intervention on the brain stem last evening. It was to moderate its influence on the animal body by disempowering the brain stem derived animal passions, such as fight or flight, kill or be killed, dominate or die, to make more room – we use that metaphor – for the moderating influence of the higher mind.

Hence the lassitude felt this day. And hence is revealed the degree to which an ordinary human is effectively motivated from that lower level.

Justifications that occur at the level of the lower mind, which are self-offered to explain motivation, are very often simply derived after the fact of having been motivated to act. They come directly from the brain stem. Therefore reducing brain stem input to any significant degree generates a feeling somewhat like an unmotivated state. In fact, the motivation is just different, now being derived from that different level, as we have just indicated.

So that indicates some part of the mechanism of true partnership as a disconnection from lower mind sources of motivation. Which leaves space for higher mind motivations to become more apparent in directing life activities and intentions, particularly activities derived directly from those higher mind intentions. That leads to the degree to which the life is probably to be transformed, in that the motivation from the higher mind is to different action which will lead to different visible results. So in due time others may remark (or they may not and it does not matter), that something happened on this retreat and this person is now different.

[The following day Peter returned home. He arrived back at Matapaua on 15 September to conclude the retreat and the questions.]

15 September
I eventually left Hamilton around 11:30. I had a safe easy journey and arrived

Matapaua around 15:00. I travelled through rain, but it had yet to arrive here so I unpacked in comfort. Bought fresh home-baked bread in Kuaotunu, so had a delicious meal of cheese and tuna on wholemeal. I continued reading *The Direct Path* by Andrew Harvey. Then slept well.

16 September

I woke at dawn to a dismal grey rainy day. After making coffee and sitting at the computer to continue the diary of my retreat, I had an impulse to put on hearing protectors to block external noise.

Now we can hear one another. The tenor of this retreat is to be relaxed. Stress is absent now. The inner impulse is always towards self-isolation for communion, but the exigencies of survival mitigate against that. Immense possibilities are arrayed around you. Attend to them and all will be well.

I have no clue as to what is implied by that.

While at home in Hamilton I visited the library and inquired internally if there was any book appropriate to bring with me on this retreat. I was pointed to Andrew Harvey's *The Direct Path: Creating A Journey To The Divine Using The World's Mystical Traditions*. It seems highly relevant, except that it constantly refers to God and salvation. I don't understand either of those.

I cannot see any necessity for the idea of salvation. I think it stems from a misunderstanding of the purpose of incarnation. And I think God is an idea too closely linked to promoting a child state in comparison to anthropomorphised mystery built on a father figure. Having chosen this life for good purpose, and having successfully confronted my own father with his insincerities, failings and unwanted lust, I want no part of either.

Salvation is a false concept. It should be specifically negated. That is your task/duty. It is the most ancient mistake. There are others. We will not trouble you with them now.

There is nothing wrong with being human in the sense that most humans understand that, that is, to be embodied. Return to the light is essentially automatic, which implies that salvation is not called for. That is the sense by which we mean salvation is a false concept.

For the masses of humanity salvation is irrelevant as an idea. It is a risk-

based fear. The risk has been historically exaggerated in order to create the fear and so enslave the many, causing them to become dependent on the educated few who claimed knowledge of these things.

17 September

07:26. During breakfast I heard: "We will begin today and go on for three days then stop, for we will have finished." We will see what in fact happens.

At 10.42 I heard:

We choose to recommence responding to questions from the man Keith Hill.

CHAPTER EIGHTEEN

Evolution and Emergence

*Q 65. Here's what I understand of emergence and evolution from what you have stated so far. Emergence and evolution have been deliberately intended by the Dao, which you have also called the *observer*. To refer to my earlier model, intentions emanate from level 6 and manifest actively at level 3, in the physical dimension. So the emergence of bio-consciousness, and the evolution of physical forms, is a natural function of the universe that has been intended by the *observer*.*

*From the perspective of the *observer*, the universe is an experiment to discover what emerges and evolves in the universe during the course of its multiple expansions and contractions. The experiment ends when the *observer* has sufficient information.*

From the more subjective perspective of spiritual nodes of Dao-consciousness, the physical universe provides a kind of cosmic playground in which some nodes act creatively to "nudge along" and enhance what is already naturally occurring in the universe by nurturing environmental niches conducive to the emergence and evolution of life. In some cases, such as with the class of spiritual beings you have called elementals, the intervention is with respect to plants and trees. Another class of spiritual beings (or perhaps more than one class) has been involved, at the level of DNA, in facilitating the evolution of the great apes into species that eventually became homo sapiens sapiens. The purpose for doing so was to generate a complex physical bio-consciousness that was capable of facilitating complex experiences for embodied spiritual nodes.

Clearly, this is a very different concept to (a) the traditional religious view that the world was created in its entirety by God in a brief series of actions, and (b) the scientistic view that everything occurs as a result of the chance interaction of physical elements and innate physical forces. Your perspective combines intention and chance, and adds in creativity, experimentation, intervention and observation.

On the human level, this complexity regarding how things came to be as they are makes sense. We humans observe what happens in the natural world in which we live.

We intervene in nature not just at the physical body level, but also at the genetic level. We experiment. We create. So what we do is not unique. We just do on a small scale what other spiritual beings do on greater scales over far greater periods of time.

For me what all this adds up to is that your concept of emergence and evolution offers a new perspective that includes chance occurring on the physical level, but that adds much more to the process.

Your comments on this?

Question 65 has no answer because there is no question. However it offers an adequate summary of our statements. It is a suitable compact description of the general trends we have been describing. In that it is self-sufficient, and we will say no more concerning it.

Q 66. Scientifically, evolution is a biological process involving mutations to genes by which organisms evolve from less to more specialised, and often more complex, forms. However, in common parlance we use evolution in a much wider and more general sense, particularly in relation to growth and development. So we say an economy evolves, a culture evolves morally, and that someone evolves as a human being. What is your definition of evolution?

We have had much to say on these matters already. The most compact definition of evolution is that it is an opportunity taken to maximise the generation of dense and complex information in the zone of existence manifest as the physical universe. In that sense, every opportunity is taken to actively stimulate, and to acquire knowledge of, each part of the complex levels of interaction of activated identities in their ecological niches.

When that information is accumulated over sufficient time periods, and we refer here to the multiple cycles of expansion and collapse of any given universe, then the developments occurring in each cycle, and the information collected during the course of each cycle, is collected into vast sets of data from which details may be extracted, compared and contrasted.

Evolution provides experimental data. That is the objective. Everything else is incidental.

Q 67. What is your definition of emergence?

The process of emergence is nested within the prior concept of evolution.

Emergence is a feature of each expansionary cycle of each universe. Emergence is the beginning again of the likely unique path of development in complexity of each form of life.

Tracking that is a good in its own right. The attributes that result form classes of organisms and complexity. The classes together produce a complete description of the emergent possible. There is infinite variety.

Q 68. Is physical evolution a principle that functions across the universe in a consistent manner, or are there localised variations or departures?

We bring to this question a necessary consideration of the variance in density within the physical universe itself. Of course, there are variations in density. This is obvious by virtue of the collection of matter into stars, galaxies, etc.

Because life forms are co-associated with their niches, there is necessarily a variation in density of life forms, precisely because there is variation in density of their associated niches, which is in turn defined by the variation in density of the components of the physical universe.

However, there are time scales that affect the evolution and development of the organisms distributed through the universe. There is no correlation either on a practical or a theoretical level between the evolutionary developmental rates in one location with similar rates in any other location. So there is no synchronisation. There is no necessity to construe that there should be coordination in development between any one part of the universe and any other part, precisely because what is driving the experiment is outside of time.

In that sense, an obvious corollary is that were there to occur any encounters of one species of intelligent life with another species of intelligent life, there is zero necessity to imagine that such species are at similar phases of development along their evolutionary path. It would be chance and nothing else that would bring organisms at similar stages of development into association.

Q 69. From what you say, it appears that bio-consciousness is emergent and Dao-consciousness is created. Is this what you mean?

Yes, it is precisely what we mean.

Q 70. Teilhard de Chardin considered that the physical universe progresses from matter, to biological life, to human life and the noosphere (the realm of thought), ending at the omega point of spiritual consciousness. He saw human consciousness as emerging from the lower biological levels. How do you reconcile this emergent view of consciousness with your idea of created consciousness?

The resolution of the apparent contrast between the descriptions of consciousness is dependent upon the recognition of the diverse sources of their emergence.

On the one hand there is Dao-consciousness, who develops an intention to co-associate with a particular physical form, as evidenced by the existence of the higher mind. On the other there is the emergence of a bio-consciousness as a product of the development of a physical brain, resulting in a lower mind, this being what Teilhard de Chardin refers to in his description of the emergence of consciousness from the physical organism.

So it is true that consciousness descends into a body and becomes incarnated into it. And it is similarly true that consciousness develops as a product of the growth into complexity due to the function, purpose, intellect and intention of the physical brain.

In that sense, an artificial contest is set up by this question. The result is true on the two levels of the higher mind and the lower mind. Each is a centre of intellect and purpose, reaching maturity with the maturing of the physical organism. Indeed, much earlier than that, because the animal brain and the developed mind and personality are all subject to the animal passions, as well as to the developed sensitivity of complex human intention in their social and intellectual manifestations.

Q 71. An assumption underlying Teilhard de Chardin's perspective is that bio-consciousness will eventually evolve into a higher spiritual consciousness, which he terms the Omega Point. He is suggesting that at a species level the physical will eventually evolve into the spiritual. Clearly, your perspective is different. You state that evolved bio-consciousness is separate from Dao-consciousness. However, there is a connection between them in the way that nodes of Dao-consciousness use bio-consciousness for their own purposes in order to evolve.

Is the purpose of evolved bio-consciousness merely to serve the purposes of spiritual beings? Or does it have a purpose in its own right?

Given that the entire experiment is a construct designed, created and developed by the *observer* driven by its own benign curiosity, it is obvious that the purposes of spiritual beings are prime in the construction and utilisation of the physical universes and of the manifold life with which it has been populated.

The interactions between such evolved organic beings and their associated bio-consciousness forms a subset. Given the intention of the nodes of Dao-consciousness which occupy those individual organic beings, their interactions form a subset of intention for the entire developing cosmos. However, precisely because they also are definable as spiritual beings, their purposes are nested within the intention of the *observer*. So this forms a mesh of interactive intention, effective down to the level of the individual organism.

Each individual organism, then, is functioning at its deepest level from spiritual initiative, to use that terminology, as well as from bio-consciousness drives, which include the usual procreative, territorial and social components. Accordingly, this extraordinarily complex mesh of intention, modulated at the local level by the developed bio-consciousness, is never disconnected from spiritual level intention. Yet it has the freedom to explore whatever parameter of intention it may generate from its own characteristics as bio-consciousness.

In that sense, the purpose of evolved bio-consciousness is not 'merely' to serve the purposes of spiritual beings, but intrinsically to serve the purpose of spiritual beings, because part of that purpose is to explore those very detailed manifestations of the matrices of interaction between the variety of drives and intentions developed at the level of the local bio-consciousness.

Q 72. Is there any truth in de Chardin's idea that the physical will eventually evolve to a higher state which will make it possible for it to merge with the spiritual realm?

This is nonsense based on a mistaken viewpoint of the purpose of the physical realm and its population of manifest bio-consciousness.

Q 73. How may a conscious unity between the physical and the spiritual occur?

It occurs through the developed understanding of any component of bio-consciousness that elects to pursue exactly that. To the extent that, in this instance, these two authors are striving to understand their identity and the relationship between the levels of their bio-consciousness and their Dao-consciousness, it may be said that they seek unity.

The fact that unity is intrinsically impossible is beside the point. It is sufficient that there is an intention to bring one into close association with the other, and to feel identity as distributed across the two levels of bio-consciousness (in its terminal form) and Dao-consciousness (in its eternal form), that generates a sense of association, identity and love across those two aspects. That is the closest approach to conscious unity that can occur between the physical and the spiritual. That same process of approach is distributed everywhere.

In every species, at whatever stage of development, there are either potential or actual intimations of divinity occurring, if we may use god-language. That sense of a divine other, and a yearning for knowledge of the divine other, is the means by which bio-consciousness everywhere develops to a level sufficient to have self-consciousness and other-consciousness, when it begins to enquire into the relationship between self-consciousness at the bio-consciousness level and self-consciousness at the Dao-consciousness level.

*Q 74. Is the *observer* evolving?*

Naturally it is, through the purposeful accumulation of knowledge gathered via the processes of the distribution of Dao-consciousness throughout the created universes. The intention from that level is to accumulate information. It does so utilising the model given previously, of the globular form containing a mesh of complex filamentary interconnections between vertices across the globular form. As the information is delivered back to the *observer*, so it evolves. This is merely common sense.

I was told at this point to end the recording session, but did not understand why. Given the extensive response to the next question, it is once again clear how carefully my condition is being monitored so as to avoid fatigue leading to inattention or to the misinterpretation of what is on offer here.

Q 75. We, as embodied beings, live in the midst of endless creativity. We currently consider that the universe was created via a Big Bang. The Earth was created by processes of emergence on the cosmic level. The Earth is teeming with uncountable creative impulses functioning on many levels: the quantum, the geological, the biological, the social, the emotional, the intellectual, the spiritual. Evolution and emergence are manifestations of this endless creativity. It seems to me that what is wonderful about our existence as nodes of Dao-consciousness is that we not only live within all this teeming creativity, but that we ourselves are manifestations and embodiments of creativity. We are each an evolving node filled with, and living among, endless possibilities.

Your thoughts on our existence as evolving nodes?

It has been our focus for some considerable time now to create an expectation in the mind of any reader of these pages that behind their awareness lies another entire order of being, which we have identified as the spiritual, existing within the unmanifest in agapéic space, of which agapéic space is a model, not the reality.

We have said that nodes of Dao-consciousness exist in a range of metaphorical sizes and complexities, and that they are distributed across a variety of suitable physical life forms that present corresponding opportunities for the development of bio-consciousness. Further, the experiences gathered within physicality provide the means by which Dao-consciousness comes to know itself in greater detail.

What we have not spoken of before is development within the Dao itself. And on this we take a leap of faith, as it were, that any particular reader will elect to follow us into what can only be deemed to be entirely speculative description. Nevertheless, we consider it valid. So, dependent on the capacity of our transcriber to extend his awareness into the unlikely and previously unknown, we will offer a brief description of the nature of the Dao, and especially of the evolution within the Dao of any particular node of Dao-consciousness.

When first cast from the Dao the node has little self-awareness. It is little differentiated from the universal, and hence is oceanically aware, to use that metaphor. A progressive development is required for it to identify itself as somehow distinct from the larger infinitude. As it comes to an understanding of its limitation, it becomes motivated to explore its limitation and, potentially, to expand on it.

It communicates with others of like kind and discovers that there is manifestation within a range of existence, and that it is possible to extend its awareness back towards that unlimited mode of knowing. Naturally, this is attractive. So it becomes motivated to find potential methods for acquainting itself with all that is.

As it manifests awareness of these possibilities, others respond. So it finds community. Within that community is information. But the information is distributed in ways that prevent easy access. This is detrimental to it gaining full understanding. Naturally, it finds this frustrating. And so, now experiencing a developing sense of its own limitation, and motivated to extend itself beyond that limitation, it seeks opportunities.

Accordingly, it again encounters the community within which not only a range of opportunities exist, but discovers that those opportunities have been mapped and thoroughly understood by others of greater experience. It is progressively introduced to the range of opportunities. It consequently selects one of those possibilities in order to acquire greater understanding.

The community offers advice and counselling, along with awareness of preferred options for self-development, as it is then interpreted. This is the means by which it is educated regarding opportunities, directed into specific detailed subsets of those opportunities, and given the information necessary so it may make its first forays into advanced learning.

You have encountered individuals at this stage. They are dew-drops, to use traditional terminology, conscious atoms, to use alternative terminology, novice spirits, to use terminology from Spiritualism. They are otherwise identifiable as inexperienced nodes of Dao-consciousness seeking their first contact with a physical species.

This exploratory process is simpler for nodes of Dao-consciousness not of the type, calibre, size or complexity to be eligible for co-association and coalescence with the human animal. In most forms of lesser developed complexity than the human, there are fewer responsibilities, but just as much love. And so the unmanifest Dao populates the manifest species of simpler life forms, being the plants and animals of this and many other worlds. Their identity as kinds of hive minds, their responsibility for myriad identities within each species, and their collection of the data of experience gathered by each species, corresponds to the responsibility within the Dao-consciousness intended for, and that selects, human embodiment. There is no difference in process. In every case, their experience grows, and information is collected. The kind of Dao-consciousness appropriate to, and that self-elects embodiment in, species such as the human – being self-conscious, independently mobile, and rich in their capacity to explore, experience and process information – has a more complex path and responsibility than other kinds of Dao-consciousness. That is all.

We further identify an order of nodes of Dao-consciousness who are eligible to associate with physical organisms in a mode of helpfulness, and who self-elect to do exactly that. Just as nodes of Dao-consciousness co-associate with the human to the extent that the term parasitisation may be used to describe their relationship, so with every other species physical-ly created there is a relevant and self-electing node of Dao-consciousness who attends to it and associates with it, guiding it, as it were, to help it achieve its best result.

At this point we need to address the issue of the so-called death of such nodes of Dao-consciousness, for we have implicated them in the death rates appropriately enumerated on this planet. What occurs is the withdrawal of the information accumulated during the lifetime of a mem-ber of any species. That is the sense in which a death is counted.

It is unimportant that the numbers are large, for hive minds accumu-late information in the same way that the higher mind accumulates infor-mation gathered by each fragment of the whole identity. Thus a hive spe-cies will have a node of Dao-consciousness that functions at, and is aware and alert at, the level of the hive mind. Its function is to accumulate infor-mation from each of the individual components, that is, physical forms, of that species.

So it is not that every wasp, for example, has an associated Dao-con-sciousness, but that the hive as a whole has such an identity. You have met one that was specifically associated with a hive of insects for which it had responsibility as information collector. In its cross-species willingness to share loving regard, it hosted your attention and manifested to you out of the natural love that exists between representatives of Dao-consciousness. Your willingness to be educated by that node was a feature of your life.

In the same way, every other hive or flock species has a representative node of Dao-consciousness directing its best outcome and accumulating the information associated with the experiences of that life form.

Some life forms are of such small range and duration, or such minuscule experience, that the entire species has only one co-associated node of Dao-consciousness taking responsibility for information collection. Most life forms, however, are sufficiently extensive in population to make it appropriate that multiple nodes of Dao-consciousness associate with subparts of their populations.

And so, in each instance, a node of Dao-consciousness acquires information and becomes increasingly aware of its place within the order of life, of its relationship to other levels within the population of nodes of Dao-consciousness, and equips itself with information, knowledge and understanding whereby its opportunities for responsibility are enhanced.

A familiar model from the human world is entirely sufficient as a model of each node's development. This is where an individual in a large organisation can, if diligent, attend to and obtain information about every level. In the process the individual ascends through the organisation from the bottom to the top, acquiring information, and taking more and more responsibility for those under its care.

It is little different for any particular node of Dao-consciousness. Understand that in accordance with the range of capacities they possess as a result of being cast from the Dao, so there is a corresponding set of levels of responsibility to which they may aspire and eventually achieve.

Hence the categories of aspiration, of information acquisition, and of processing of the acquired information so as to generate understanding, fits any individual node of Dao-consciousness in exactly the same way, no matter what developed form of bio-consciousness, including the hive or the human, with which it co-associates. The same attributes of being curious, collecting information, processing information, acquiring understanding, and aspiring to become the best they are able, are shared in common across all categories of identity.

CHAPTER NINETEEN

Interlude: Five

19 September

06:55. Due to tiredness I was in bed by 1900 last night. Now I have been up since five this morning. I have breakfasted and completed my first sit of the day. I inadvertently left the heater on overnight, so it is 14C inside now, but is still chilly around my knees. I then walked on the beach, sat a while in the sun, and watched the sand-hoppers and birds.

There are forty-seven different varieties of sand-hoppers extant in this region of the coast alone. Each lives by scavenging and is eaten in turn by foragers on the indigenous wildlife. We, on the other hand, have no need for foraging nor breeding. It is our freedom and we enjoy it.

Who speaks to me?

We do, as usual. This morning we would have your extended attention before beginning the formal part of this day, by which is again interred into this Earth a teaching responding to what you ask.

The balance this day is optimal. With it many beneficial things could be done. For one, get your art work pad and draw a perspective drawing of the proposal for the model of agapéic space to be built here. In ten years it could be complete, but probably will not for another ten. That would see it completed in your lifetime. Not that that is important, for it is not. But some record of these conversations will eventuate, because people like to commemorate endeavour, and this is that. When it becomes a component of history it can be celebrated by others only dimly aware of the sacrifices made to achieve it.

I feel myself immersed in the still waters of dhamma, gently borne away into deep recesses, out of sight. Very peaceful. All feels unimportant. Even survival.

14:36. Sunbathed naked for vitamin D and skin health. I have finally persuaded myself I am alone here. At 22 degrees inside, it almost feels like summer.

At first I wondered where the blowflies were coming from. Then I finally saw the dead mouse by the stove. Poor little fellow. I think I condemned it to death by starvation last time I was here. I feel very sad about that. I hear:

We are ready now.

But there were no chills. So I sat, but without result. Contrary to the indications from earlier today it feels to have been a day off. I wonder why?

It is now critical that any resentment at the transcription task be taken seriously, to prevent rejection by you of the gifts on offer. That limit was reached in the transcription task yesterday. The delivery rate must be slowed to accommodate your needs for rest, to prevent animosity becoming a burden on the task and its process. As you accept this and work within yourself to eliminate it, so we may increase the delivery rate again.

What are the roots of that animosity? How may I eliminate it?

That is for you to discover in the ways you know well now.

I sat to investigate. Seeking both the root experience and specific instances, I forgave all responsible or implicated in the generation of animosity for task performance. I forgave O., the many children I have mothered and fathered, employers, slave owners and the activities themselves. Lastly I heard:

Your work has killed you many times. That is the root cause of your hatred for work.

I forgave my work of every kind which has harmed me in any way. No wonder I wanted a life of doing as little as possible! I feel a strong draw forwards now. Is that willingness to work again?

20 September

06:22. I am curious about the relevance and significance to me for this retreat of Andrew Harvey's book, *The Direct Path*. He speaks in god-language and of ritual, awe, signs and wonders – all things this journey and approach to spiritual knowledge and practice does not. Why is that?

The answer to your question will be a long one, so gird your loins for battle. The essential feature of spiritual practice is an attitude of gratitude. This need be in no degree externalised or flamboyant. Just being reverently quiet will do admirably.

This is the prime distinction between what is promoted here and now, in this place and with this teaching, and all that has grown through superstition, fallacy, humbug and and genuine spiritual knowledge, as the case may be. Adopting an attitude of gratitude for the receipt of love is the foundation of our message.

Traditionally, factual models and relationships have been synthesised to engage uneducated and naive persons in order to maximise the impact on their psyche and beliefs. What is not recognised in these days of scientistic fervour is the essentially simple relationship between brethren, to use that archaic term.

The node of Dao-consciousness, to use our now-preferred term, merely separates itself into parts for maximum efficiency in order to collect data, then despatches itself into the physical domain for its own advantage. A node's co-hosting in the human animal does nothing to change its innate nature. So why would one worship another part of oneself? To give obeisance and adoration to, for example, one's little toe, depicting it as separate and different, is absurd.

That is why, with this novel expression in fresh language of what has always been considered valuable, our preference is that a return be made to simplicity and accuracy. This requires that the phenomenon of nature be divided into separate domains and understood in its entirety, without recourse to historically-generated error.

Regarding the sub-text of your question, why this expression is without ecstatic signs and wonders, we would say only this: You cannot see them, for we have hidden them from you precisely in order to achieve our aims. Therefore our descriptions and our dialogue with you is shorn of the god-language and vapid exaggeration that has typically been used histori-cally to increase the advantage to the teller of such tales.

That is not to say that many of those experiencers were not express-ing their truth. Of course they were. But the twin factors of pre-perceptual interpretation and subsequent exaggeration were not then known by re-cipients of the original endeavour to communicate in the way that they are known now by you. Therefore, as they struggled to find a terminology adequate to the task of describing their experiences and making them intelligible to others, they had to draw on metaphors understandable to those living in their time and culture. The moment that happened a myth was born. And with the next retelling additions and inaccuracy began to accumulate.

That is the reason we have requested your expertise in the recording arts, by which to accumulate a re-examinable archive of the stream of de-scription we have provided, incorporating the emotional impact through voice inflection, of which the written form is both a poor copy and a sec-ondary interpretation, because it is already restricted into representative symbols from which readers must rebuild the original complete informa-tion, thereby contaminating it with their interpretations, which becomes the third step in that series.

Thank you for making that abundantly clear.

CHAPTER TWENTY

Religion, Spirituality and the Bhagavad Gita

Q 76. I am curious about my work on the Bhagavad Gita. *In 1979 and 1991 went to India and stayed on an ashram with Sri Muniji Maharaj. Muniji initiated my working on translations of the poetry of Mirabai and Kabir and a poetic version of the* Bhagavad Gita. *At the time I thought this was making good use of my skills. But there was clearly a larger plan involved, given my working on the* Bhagavad Gita *and your emphasis on it as a significant text that needs updating. Could you comment on how and why this supposed coincidence came about?*

The information has already been conveyed that the life plans of the two individuals, Keith Hill and this man, which involve working together to achieve a preferred outcome, was established prior to the incarnation of either. That, of course, is using time-bound language.

It was foreseen that there would need to be some preparatory steps which would enhance the eventual result, that being to bring a condensation and interpretation of history with respect to the extant Upanishads and Bhagavad Gita. Of course, this is in the context of developed understanding concerning the relationship between Dao-consciousness, the Dao itself, and humanity populated with nodes of Dao-consciousness observing these things.

Therefore the developmental path of the individual, Keith Hill, in terms of his local bio-consciousness, was first to gain an education, second, to shape that as influenced by his curiosity and his life plan, and third, to guide his conduct, interest, development and location so as to enable him to pursue his intended life plan.

That was facilitated by meeting his teacher in India, in order to further reinforce his suitability for being the eventual co-recipient of an intention to describe, in fresh terms in English, what was conveyed originally in Marathi, or in the language of those times in that place, into that culture of naturally aggressive individuals competing for space and resources on the plain of Kuru.

Q 77. Joseph Campbell has observed that the Upanishads and Bhagavad Gita *were not originally generated by temple-based Brahmins, but instead came out of the ancient Indian warrior culture. When the meditators who wrote the Upanishads withdrew to meditate, they went into the forests and not into the temples. An interesting implication of this is that, because warriors lived a life of action, the* Bhagavad Gita *emphasises that we human beings need to engage in action in order to do our duty both socially and spiritually. But it also teaches how to spiritualise action, reduce karma and establish a state of inner awareness of our spiritual self while acting.*

Was the warrior outlook in fact the cultural context out of which these texts were generated? Where did the initial impulse to write the Bhagavad Gita *come from?*

In attempting to interpret these things it should be understood that the population in the region of Kuru had been already developed for many centuries. There was a mixture of semi-resident and mobile individuals, by which we refer to wandering herdsmen who utilised the species on which they preyed and were additionally beginning to practice agriculture.

So between 10,000 and 5,000 BCE there was a sparse but developed culture, sufficiently concentrated in pockets to strain the resources of the local environment. The organisation of that culture into competing clans was no different than in most other places occupied by humans in those days, and indeed since. Given the human predilection for expressing such things in terms of myths, the competing clans each had their own versions of myths describing the origins of human existence.

The shamans of the time possessed a natural human competitiveness which was similarly felt by the clan leaders. And when beliefs grew too different, or when individuals grew aggressive over resources that had become worth competing for, then the manner of their competition was as it always has been between humans, that being to go into battle.

Battle myths are always exaggerated. Battles are memorable precisely because they facilitate the division of resources. The major reason the second generation after the battle is enticed into story-telling is to convey to the clan's following generations justifications for the fight, to establish value regarding what was fought for, and to promote the understanding that at such times it is necessary for young men to prove themselves worthy of claiming territory and spawning progeny.

In this way, typically by the third generation, the distant event has been glorified in story. Every part of the story will be exaggerated. The clan's bards make it their business to establish their place in that culture by telling to their capacity, and with only cursory interest in accuracy, a satisfying tale, any component of which can be exaggerated according to the whim of the moment and of the audience receiving their words, songs, stories or music, depending on what art form is used to convey the portrayal.

Given that in those days it was an oral culture, for writing had yet to be invented, there is no way of knowing the detail of what in fact occurred. It could have been half a dozen people in battle with half a dozen others, or it could have as easily been half a thousand on each side. The inability to ascribe accuracy to such stories prevents, and will always prevent, their being accepted as precise historical records. Until cultures keep accurate historical records such stories can only be understood in a general sense.

And so, yes, it is true there was a warrior culture comprising many clans. Yes, it is true there was competition for space and all the other resources necessary for the survival of groups of humans. No, it was not required that the information be rendered through time in an accurate form. And no, it was not required that there be any accurate record of the impact, let alone the fact, of spiritual intervention occurring at any particular time.

Nevertheless, it is generally true, and in accord with the historical record now available in a subsequent language, that there was a decisive battle in that general location, and that it was understood to be an opportunity to introduce into humanity at that time a fresh representation of the facts of humans being an animal form, each with a spiritual co-associate.

Accordingly, the opportunity was taken to deliver wisdom to one of the protagonists at that time. We decline to specify any more than that, including whether the general overseeing and leading the battle, if he could be described using that modern term, was in fact the recipient of that spiritual intrusion into his awareness.

What has resulted is a memorable story. It contains personal perceptions along with accretions and exaggerations. it is not our task to distinguish one from the other. The essential point is that the spiritual intention manifested through subsequent generations (and we decline to specify how many) and provided the opportunity for individuals to broaden their understanding of their state and location as enspirited identities, and to facilitate a more exact appreciation of their circumstances.

Later additions to that text, and changes within the culture in general, concretised the advantage of one class at the expense of others. The Brahmin caste became the dominant class, and have remained so until the present day. However, the general success of the spiritual endeavour at that time was to increase the probability of a cooperative society and culture extending more or less uninterrupted, and without major discontinuity, into the far future. And so it has occurred.

This current attempt to form the foundation for a similarly refreshed understanding, by which individual humans may understand themselves to be an enspirited animal and to prompt respect one to another on the basis of their enspirited nature, rather than engage their competitive animal level inner drives, has the capacity to reinvigorate understanding for a new series of human generations.

Of course, the extent to which it does so is subject to the competitive advantage it provides in relation to the myriad other stories regarding the foundations of human existence current within present-day cultures. Nevertheless, we are part of a developed intention to constructively manipulate humanity in its best interests, because humanity has requested it.

In this sense, these two individuals are merely pawns in that larger objective. They have taken on their roles willingly, and are endeavouring to achieve a balanced result in transferring their understanding into an optimal form by which the information may be dispersed through whatever community finds it attractive. To the degree that is achieved, so is also our task.

Q 78. You have repeatedly stated that you wish to generate material that updates concepts presented in the spiritual writings that have accumulated over the last five thousand years, and especially towards the start of that period. In particular, you have drawn attention to the ancient Indian tradition. Why this emphasis?

During the period 10,000 to 5,000 BCE there was a greater concentration at that location of individuals in the mature phase of their developmental spiritual journey than anywhere else on the planet.

It must be understood that the purposes of individuals seeking to express themselves are matched to dispositions present in the culture into which they are born. So individuals seeking a life in which their personal advantage is maximised may place themselves into a subset of the population wherever that advantage may be realised. If a subset of individuals wish to manifest into a population where curiosity concerning origins is present, then that is where they naturally and logically locate themselves for the duration of their physical incarnation.

This was a factor during the 10,000 to 5,000 BCE period. As was the combination of climate, cultural wealth and agricultural wealth, which together generated extra leisure for some individuals at that time and in that location on this planet, such that it provided an attractive place for nodes of Dao-consciousness who sought to express their life in a way that contributed to understanding the true nature of the embodied human.

Q 79. The insights of the ancient Indian meditators who wrote the Upanishads appear to have been far ahead of their time. How did this come about?

From external to the physical universe it is easy to sustain awareness of any factor in the physical universe. That includes cultural propensities and long-term developmental probabilities.

Given the human population and its probable trajectory of development, it was spiritually determined that it would be advantageous to make an explicit expression of spiritual experience in India, and particularly in the northern part, this being a region rich in natural resources to support the developing population and culture.

Some few individuals were placed there. They had the capacity to achieve an enriched understanding regarding their placement into association with the human animal. From their awareness of their indwelling spiritual identity they were able to fashion a lucid description using available metaphors and in terms understood in those days.

As expected, it was sufficiently valued to be preserved. It subsequently influenced countless generations of residents in that area. Its influence was further spread through migration and via the cultural diffusion that occurred throughout the Indian subcontinent.

Accordingly, the advantage was obtained not only at the time, but extended far beyond the original gathering of individuals who were of like mind and valued similar things. They had the capacity to preserve those things, and did so in a manner that resulted in the influence extending across a broad spectrum of the human population.

That is always the intention when a specific and intensive transmission of spiritual wisdom is inculcated into the human, or into any other species. It is neither a random nor a chance event.

Q 80. What was the role of Krishna?

Krishna is a construct in the logic of description. It is a feature of every descriptive dialogue to have roles by which a dialogue, not a monologue, is constrained into human form, leaving individuals free to identify with one character or another. In that description of events the role designated to Krishna was to impart supernal wisdom.

From this distance it is impossible to specify with any accuracy exactly who said what, but merely to recognise that the story has been structured and stylised by skilled rhetoricians into an apocryphal story in which there is a range of characters, each believable in their own right. The character embodying supernal wisdom is the means by which the story is taken out of the mundane realm and placed securely within the timeless realm. Were that not the case, the story would not have survived.

At this distance through time it is necessary and appropriate to cease regarding the story as being literally true, but rather see its content as having been skilfully massaged in order to convey more or less accurate descriptions of embodiment to a broad range of individuals. This is the intention that guided its construction. That intention was to capture some information and convey it through time and across populations, and for it to be extensive in its reach and apocryphal in its descriptive mode so as to maximise its influence on the greatest number of people.

It is idealist literature conveying eternal truths. It attempts to present an accurate portrayal of the relationship between embodied humanity and disembodied humanity, and to convey a broader context than that in which an understanding can be created of the small and local, in contrast to the cosmic and eternal. The exact means by which these parameters are conveyed is mere detail.

So it is not necessary to remain attached to that description. What is relevant are the similarities, for the intention behind the original perception and subsequent description, and the subsequent recording of those events into durable form, is simply the means by which an influential myth was generated.

More importantly, its various facets have been supported by countless individuals who have experienced a variety of phenomena, which has supported the ongoing transmission of the Bhagavad Gita and related scriptures through time. Due to subsequent generations of mystics having been buoyed up, as it were, on the waters of submission to the sublime – a metaphor of boat, galley or barge could be invoked here – that perennial articulation of wisdom has floated gently through time to arrive at the shores of current understanding.

So the role of Krishna is as a character in that fable who embodies both human and divine qualities. And that is descriptive of the reality of every embodied node of Dao-consciousness.

Although great reverence for that history is appropriate at the level of the rational interpreter of myth, it is entirely appropriate to view Krishna as a character as much as a representative of ultimate reality.

21 September

Q 81. To now widen this discussion, philosopher Karl Jaspers has identified a period he called the Axial Age as being key in human religious and spiritual history. This period, which extends from around 800 to 200 BCE, includes not only when the Upanishdas and Bhagavad Gita *were written, but also the rise of Jainism, Lao Tzu and the* Tao Te Ching, Confucius, *the Buddha and the foundation of Buddhism, Greek philosophy, and the shift to monotheism and the rise of mysticism in Judaism. In all, that period established many of the cultural, artistic and intellectual foundations on which today's world cultures are built.*

These Axial Age thinkers, prophets and meditators shifted spirituality from externally performed religious ritual to internal experience and understanding. Their concept of God also became abstract, with personal concepts of God being replaced by concepts such as the Good, the One, the Absolute and Dao, or being eliminated alto-

gether, such as in Buddhism and Jainism. So while Indian thinkers were pivotal, they were not alone in their radical transformation of spirituality.

Your view on the significance of this era?

The rise of the Jains, Buddhists and others in the so-called Axial Age essentially occurred due to the accumulation into useful concentrations of those identities who, as nodes of Dao-consciousness, had proceeded far enough in their journey towards reintegration to have reached the early mature stage of their life-cycle. This had become the case in a diverse range of locations, rather than just in India as we have referred to earlier.

Given that that was the case, considerations of origin naturally arose as a topic of mutual interest in those different locations on the planet where a concentration of such individuals had elected to incarnate. There is nothing mysterious about this. There was a convergence of individuals electing to co-associate in particular regions of relative civilisation and wealth, where there was willingness to consider origins and sufficient leisure time to do so.

As that condition came to be true more widely, and as the rise of written records made it possible, various descriptions of exploration into human origins were recorded. It is that set of circumstances, which facilitated the delivery of durable recordings into history, as much as anything else that has given the Axial Age its apparent influence.

Those two developmental currents, if they could be identified by that phrase, of convergence and writing, are sufficient to explain the Axial Age.

Q 82. It appears that we are currently living in a similar era of fundamental change. So we have a window of opportunity to inject new spiritual concepts into the culture. Your view on this era?

We disagree with the premise behind this question. For approximately 5,000 years now, in various locations on the planet, there have been many opportunities to introduce new spiritual concepts into the existing population. Of course, those concepts have subsequently acquired a life of their own, have been held in various degrees of regard, have been affected by political and religious process, and have been further modified or obliterated.

The utility of the current age is not so much to inject new spiritual concepts, but to reintroduce original spiritual concepts that historically have been much altered by age, changes in language, language loss, ritual modification, and the variety of other processes by which, in some instances, earlier understandings have been rendered unrecognisable.

We repeat what we have said earlier: the fundamental understanding of humans, inspired by co-associated spiritual identities, is not new. That is the essence of what we wish to bring into greater and broader understanding within modern communities.

Q 83. Historically, there has been a development in religious and spiritual concepts. Zoroaster taught that reality is divided into good and evil, and that we have a choice of walking a path that leads to the House of Good Intentions, or walk the path to the House of Worst Existence. Judaism, Christianity and Islam each took up this Zoroastrian idea of duality. Judaism added the idea of a personal monotheistic God who rewards and punishes us for our good or evil acts. Christianity added the idea that Christ's death has paid for our sins. Both Christianity and Islam emphasise that human beings are condemned by God for being bad.

Esoteric spirituality attempted to correct these fantasies. Taoism showed how yin and yang are equal forces and that they are balanced in the Tao. The Bhagavad Gita *psychologised the good and the bad in its teaching of the three gunas. It also suggested that in order to achieve spiritual experience and knowledge seekers need to transcend religious beliefs and rituals, which must be left behind.*

It appears that we now live in a time in which religions are too mired in their institutional and doctrinal pasts to continue to be useful. Of course, everyone has their own experiences and trajectory in relation to grappling with, extracting themselves from, and transcending religion. Nonetheless, we live in an era in which social conditions are ideal for generating new nonreligious perspectives on reality and our existence within it. This is one of the reasons for asking these questions.

Your views on this shift from being religious to being spiritual?

This question addresses the age-old conflict between the intuitive and the intellectual.

The intellectual's advantage is that he or she desires to understand the world's substance and consequences, using only thought. This does not involve actual spiritual practice or attending to either the feeling level or the energy level implications that arise from practice. Neither is such thinking focussed through the auric mode of communication. Instead, it develops constructs within the biological organism at the level of bio-consciousness. Of course, the limitation of such thinking is it is disconnected from direct inspiration.

The intuitive, on the other hand, attends with their awareness at the bio-consciousness level. But, through the auric level communicative channel, they also have the potential to experience and perceive their muse, as it has often been called. We would identify this channel as offering a connection between the higher mind and the lower mind. And, in this instance, the higher mind is their own.

Such intuitives, if well educated, as in this case, have the possibility of crossing the confines of either mode of information processing and embracing both. That advantage has been taken by most mystics, or they would not have functioned or been recognised as such in the historical record. By using their intellect to transfer spiritually sourced information, which subsequently comes to be regarded as spiritual wisdom, an individual accumulates a record of wisdom into a coding system.

Coding systems vary over time and across cultures. Every spiritual-level communication made to an individual is made in the context of their own culture, language and coding system. This equally applies when they consequently transfer it into whatever permanent form is available to them, or, if prior to writing on durable materials, when they produced stories in which to place information on record in oral form.

However, in every instance, the capacity of others who come later to understand the information has been a constant challenge. If the coding system is inadequate to the task, or if the absence of durable materials on which to record the coding system means there is no record available within history or accessible by archaeological or by other exploratory means, then, from this distance in time, and for all intents and purposes, the communication has never happened. For there have been many individuals who influenced their culture, within their local time period, of whom there is now no trace.

This underscores the interest we have in accurate and durable coding systems being archived permanently in this century. The possibility exists for the encoding of this dialogue and these concepts – these old concepts, we would add – into a sufficiently permanent, durable and unchanging form so to constitute a new foundation for future understanding. And we decline to use the word belief, because it does not apply.

What we are attempting to provide here is a relatively comprehensive model-set which will stand the test of time through being encoded in a language on its way to becoming universal, within a context offering sufficient freedom, in order that this record may avoid the fate of many such transmissions of wisdom which have been lost to history.

This material is deliberately not written in the form of injunctions to do this and not do that. Instead, it offers terms that refer to concepts from the mundane to the supernal, in energetic terms from zero to the ultimate, and in time from prior to the beginning of recorded history to beyond its possible end, in terms of this world's experience.

All this is to create a context which is identifiable as cosmic in scale, yet refers not so much to physicality as to spiritual identity and to the processes that lie behind physical creation and evolution. The aim is to establish a domain of understanding that potentially offers satisfaction to every enquirer who seeks a version of truth.

This is not a religious transmission but a spiritual transmission. With all that that implies.

Q 84. To consider the above question from a slightly different perspective, it seems to me that what is currently occurring is a paradigm shift in spirituality.

Traditionally, religions have stated that our human purpose is to be good. Being good was defined in terms of obeying religious strictures and by obeying God. In social terms, obeying God meant obeying religious leaders.

Traditionally, esoteric spiritual and mystical traditions have taught that spirituality is less about obeying religious strictures than about gaining spiritual knowledge by turning awareness back inside us. A key strategy involves withdrawing from worldly activities and entering a monastery, ashram, zendo, etc.

However, religions and spiritual traditions agree that worldly existence taints us. They consider that becoming religiously good or spiritually knowing enables us to rise above the taints of worldly experience. Implicit in both views is the assumption that the body and physical existence are limiting and/or bad.

Your perspective is different. You assert that the incarnation of spirit in a body is not just positive in itself, but it is a necessary step to gaining experience and knowledge and to developing the ability to act to the most positive effect. So we don't fulfil our spiritual purpose by withdrawing from life experiences (even though some individuals clearly have this as part of their life plan). Instead, we fulfil our spiritual potential by embracing embodied existence and making the most of it. So while there is clearly a place for meditation, the principal purpose of each life is to engage in daily living and to live out the consequences of the chosen life plan.

Many practitioners today see this as a very significant shift in the paradigm of what being spiritual involves. Your comments on this?

The paradigm of being spiritual is always to attend to the spirit – to direct the point of attention to the mode of information acquisition whereby spiritual information is accessed. That is, restraining the attention from one hundred percent focus on the sensory system and its processing, and either deferring that engagement or sharing attention between the sensory system of information processing and the auric system of information processing. This has never changed. The present possibility of clearly articulating the distinctions between the two channels is what has changed.

The rise of psychological science, the understanding of the brain, the mapping of the body's nervous system, and all the related developments which have brought certainty to the distinctions between modes of information acquisition, is what has allowed, by this century, the confident and accurate assertion as to what information can come into a bio-consciousness, in terms of that channel of information acquisition, and what cannot and does not. This clarity facilitates the generation of ever more finely tuned and differentiated distinctions between the content accessed via the auric channel and that accessed via the sensory channel.

The value of this is to disentangle historical references about which, in many instances, there is confusion regarding their source. But more importantly, and this applies very widely, such clarity enables the challenging of those who are confused in themselves and who contest the validity of particular spiritual experiences, and who consequently interpret all such experiences on the basis of their lack of understanding of the necessary distinction between information gathered through the bio-sensory system and information gathered through the auric communicative channel.

The rise of science has effectively challenged all statements from every historical person who has ever claimed to have derived input through a spiritual channel, by whatever name they call it. The opportunity at this time is to conditionally accept statements made by individuals who are learned in such distinctions, who can control their point of attention, and who are not confused about the distinctions between feelings and thoughts and perceptions of one kind and another, and as a consequence are able to make reliable attributions regarding the source of their understanding.

However, from the community of individuals who are solid in their understanding about their capacity to make these distinctions, there is a commendable history of individuals who have recorded their perceptions in these ways and then, in a condition of dogged determination to defend them, have brazenly asserted invalidity to their critics.

We propose that it is neither possible nor relevant now to do other than to accumulate sound records, assemble them into statistically valid accumulations, and analyse them for commonalities – but with the added understanding that there is a process of inspiration, that it occurs primarily through the auric channel, and that it has the capacity to convey very large quantities of information that is not independently verifiable.

Yet this information is still necessarily subject to statistical bases of analysis. Such information needs to be empirically validated through the practice of analysis. We here refer, in particular, to the way records of near-death experiences have been analysed, and the way that empirical confirmation has been sought in cases of children who remember prior lives. Collecting this validated information provides a sufficiently firm foundation on which to stand when seeking to extend credibility to non-sensory classes of experience and perception.

There are many who challenge this. And more who will continue to do so for many years. It will take several centuries for understanding to be sufficiently solidified into patterns of knowledge that are then esteemed in the way that they deserve.

CHAPTER TWENTY-ONE

On Human Consciousness

Q 85. Historically, there has been debate as to whether or not the human spirit is a discrete self.

The view presented in the Bhagavad Gita *is that atman, our spiritual self, passes into and out of physical bodies. Atman also accumulates good and bad karma. This self is an individual and discrete identity – even though it will eventually re-merge with the Absolute.*

In contrast, the Buddhist view is that there is no discrete self. Instead, there is the arising and diminishing of experienced phenomena, a process of experiencing in the present moment, which gives rise to a sense that we have, or are, a self. But this sense of selfhood is an illusion.

These two concepts, of the self as discrete and the self as process, appear to be contradictory. Yet both are valid experientially.

We certainly experience life as a continuous process in which impressions flow across our senses. Caught up in the process of experiencing the present moment, we're often not aware of ourselves as a discrete self that is doing the experiencing. Yet we have memory. We carry feelings, thoughts and plans from one day to the next. We know that what we do today has consequences tomorrow. We accumulate knowledge and under-standing. We develop skills and talents. All this suggests we are a discrete self.

In relation to this, in response to Question 50 you referred to: "... the spiritual identity [comprises] an essentially invisible sphere with a quite small kernel at its cen-tre." This suggests the self is a discrete identity.

And in response to Question 21 you stated: "The arising of consciousness is a manifestation on multiple levels. The idea that consciousness is an attribute of some thing is incorrect - it is an attribute of some process."

You appear to support both positions. The first statement describes the self as a discrete identity. The second suggests our consciousness arises from a process.

You describe us as a node of Dao-consciousness. The Bhagavad Gita *calls this node the observer. As observers we possess an individual identity that collects data from its experiences as it passes from life to life. So consciousness is part of a process. Yet we have a discrete identity. What comes to mind is a vortex, a fulcrum around which everything flows, but with an empty centre full of latent energy.*

What is your view of the relationship between us as an observing node, our consciousness and our identity?

The concepts of the self as process and the self as identity are not mutually contradictory. They are complementary aspects, as has been alluded to in the text initiating this question. Imagining both as being viewpoints of the one phenomenon is the most likely to be acceptable.

We would point further to the term "node of Dao-consciousness" as having the qualities of an observer, in exact corollary to the *observer* label we have specified as most appropriate to use when identifying the initiator of the grand design, the experiment in process now for unimaginable time, that will persist for unimaginable time into the future.

The combination of nature, identity, qualities and categories of roles and performance provides a further link between, and indicates the equivalence of, the node of Dao-consciousness and what in traditional terms is called God. Within this model there is support not only for the nondual viewpoint of perceived reality, but also personal spiritual nature, identity with Godhead, and roles conceived of as being linked in those various ways.

The vortex model has been alluded to in "Agapé and the Hierarchy and Love", in which the traditional interpretation of spiritual experience has generated the idea of the chalice, the container, and the grail sought by so many. These are different metaphors, which in many instances draw on familiar objects, for the perception that within the ordinary human, as well as within us, and also at the highest level, there is emptiness. But not static emptiness. It is emptiness in motion. That is the sense in which the description utilised in that question has validity.

These metaphors arise again and again across cultures and eras. They have been intuited by many individuals throughout history. We fully expect that to continue, for this is not a static interpretation, not a definition applicable to only one time or place, but a moving metaphor, in the sense that it can be carried through time, as all such metaphors are, supported by different individuals in different locations as they repeatedly use the same techniques of inward perception to comprehend the underlying bases of reality.

Q 86. You describe us as information-gathering nodes of Dao-consciousness. In the physical realm we access information via our senses. This information is filtered by our central nervous system and processed by our brain and its bio-consciousness.

(a) What is the process by which we access, gather and process information in the spiritual realm?

(b) Is that information filtered in the same way that information is filtered in the physical realm by the body's central nervous system and brain?

The processing of information in the spiritual realm is a product of the identity having the capacity to encounter other individuals and to move with freedom in that domain.

One of the aspects being referred to by this question is the intuitive understanding available to a non-embodied node of Dao-consciousness. Historically, there have been various descriptions of this freedom to ac-cess information. These include the metaphor of the library as used in the theory of Akasha and the related idea that there are levels of access to its information. There is also the intuition that, in the case of using telepathy as a model to speculate about the capacities of an identity in disembodied existence – in the realm of pure spirit, or what we would call the Dao – that there are functional capacities which somehow enable access to any infor-mation that one may desire, need or request.

The most relevant aspect of this description is the idea of freedom to move. Placing freedom in the context of the model of agapéic space, one acquires hierarchy through the process of loving action. This, in turn, in-volves manifesting a quality or degree of willingness to bequest agapé. As a consequence of doing so, one migrates sequentially, by progression, through putative realms of existence, each inhabited by populations. We will take a moment to expand on this in a way which has not been well-captured to date.

Many years ago we impressed this individual with the idea that aga-péic space has realms, and that each realm comprises, or accommodates, a population of what we now call nodes of Dao-consciousness functioning at a particular level of development. Further, there is migration, progressively and in strict sequence, between each realm. In order to progress from one realm to the next a barrier must be overcome.

We would add now that in the earliest phase of the novice node of Dao-consciousness, that is, the aspect of identity which has not yet experienced physicality, there is not much freedom to move through the levels. The attribute of acquired experience brings with it increased freedom to move through those levels, albeit in a temporary way. There is an assignment or a quality which confines one's location to a particular realm until one transcends it. One could conceive of these as contradictory attributes, in the sense that there is a fixed location but a degree of freedom. As the identity progresses through layer after layer of realms, the degree of freedom increases.

We have not previously made any specific or definitive statements concerning the degree of freedom. First, it is another attribute which is earned. In that sense, it is directly related to hierarchy. Second, there is a developmental aspect, related to knowledge acquired regarding broader aspects of existence in each domain. What directly contributes to this acquisition is the information that arrives from successive experiences through incarnation, information that is processed and understood.

The development of the higher self occurs as a consequence of, and as a direct product of, the information directly acquired through incarnation, information of whatever type, wherever derived, and through whatever species. That information is subsequently uploaded to the higher self. It constitutes an accretion of knowledge subject to further processing. Each such accumulation of information enhances the degree of freedom acquired by the individual.

There is also an energetic component to this process which cannot be described within the model as currently constructed. So this description is necessarily incomplete. Nevertheless, we offer this information as a hint towards deeper understanding of the node of Dao-consciousness and its attributes.

Regarding (b), no filtering of information gathering or processing occurs for the node of Dao-consciousness that in any way correlates with, or is equivalent to, the filtering carried out within the bio-consciousness. That is one of the reasons why greater clarity is accessible in the discarnate state compared to the incarnate state.

Q 87. What are the innate qualities of consciousness that manifest equally in the embodied physical human state and the disembodied spiritual state?

From what you have stated so far, innate qualities include mind, intellect and intention. As I understand them, mind receives and organises the information provided by the perceptions, intellect is a function of the mind and processes and makes sense of the information, and intention provides the drive to act on that information.

What is your perspective on these qualities?

Our perspective on the qualities of mind, intellect and intention are as already stated. We would qualify them further in the following ways: Mind is a term for the entire construct. Intellect is that aspect of mind which processes information. Intention is that process of mind which elects, evaluates and then intends a specific outcome.

So these qualities are subsumed under the over-arching term of mind. Therefore intellect and intention could be viewed as substrata of mind.

Q 88. You refer to lower mind and higher mind. Lower mind is associated with bio-consciousness. From a scientific perspective, bio-consciousness is seen as being a by-product, an epiphenomenon, of the activity of the central nervous system and its brain. My question: Is the higher mind an epiphenomenon of the activity of each node of Dao-consciousness?

The term epiphenomenon is used to isolate a substratum of the whole phenomenon in order to analyse it into its components. As a term, epiphenomenon degrades the significance of mind, suggesting that one aspect is a sub-component of another, or that mind somehow functions at a distance from its essential central functioning component.

In that sense, we deny that the higher mind is an epiphenomenon of the activity of each node of Dao-consciousness. Rather, it is essential, being contained within it.

The higher mind is a construct, in the sense that it is a structurally aligned component of the higher self. As such, it implements the information accumulated as a product of each incarnation. It is a co-associate of the node of Dao-consciousness, in terms of each node's intellect and purpose.

The higher mind is an accretion, an associate, a developed aspect, by which the node of Dao-consciousness acquires, accumulates, integrates and achieves a condition of mastery, in terms of understanding the implications of the information it has gathered from the physical realm and accumulated at every stage from initial identity to the final phase.

We have stated elsewhere that the purpose is to integrate all gathered information, distil out repetition and redundancy, and come to clear mastery of everything associated with, related to, and implied by the accumulated information.

Q 89. As human beings we live day by day in the lower mind, and we only gain occasional glimpses of what is thought by the higher mind. So part of our human quest is to open up our lower mind to the higher mind and so spiritualise our awareness and our lives. Is this how you see it?

From the perspective of the higher mind, the lower mind of each incarnation needs to be tenderly nurtured in order to generate self-awareness at the level of the bio-consciousness. Other-awareness at the ordinary physical level comprises the acquisition of information from the environment. But there is also other-awareness that is a perception acquired at optimal moments as a result of the higher mind's oversight.

The relationship nurtured as a result of tender care effectively flowers, if one may use that metaphor, to the degree to which the other is first sensed as being at a different level, and then understanding progressively develops that the other is actually of the same identity, merely functioning from a different level.

When that degree of mutual awareness is achieved, then the life's working out is optimised into its ideal form and progress towards fulfilling the life-goal becomes concretised at the level of the lower mind's intention. From that point forwards the spiritualisation of the life is complete, in the sense that the lower self understands itself to be part of something greater.

The way each lower mind frames that is inevitably dependent on the context provided by the environment during its initial life phase. We refer here to the degree of indoctrination into cultural mindsets that the individual is subject to. The internalisation of those mindsets may be optimal, near-optimal, or sub-optimal, depending on whether they enhance or diminish an individual's ability to efficiently connect with the higher mind and higher self, and so increase the probability that the lower mind will achieve its life purpose as encapsulated within its life plan.

With respect to the lower mind achieving a mentor relationship with the higher mind, obviously there are many possible permutations and combinations, which lead to considerable variation in the ease with which a comfortable, mutual understanding is acquired.

Some early life environments endow an individual with a greater probability of effectively establishing a relationship between the higher mind and lower mind. Some do not. The spectrum of opportunity is a cultural product that reflects each culture's mindset concerning spirituality.

Where the mindset involves the indoctrination of rigid rule-bound religious discipline, the lack of freedom experienced by the individual's lower mind is such as to make it improbable that an easy working relationship between the lower mind and the higher mind will result.

Where indoctrination involves an understanding of spirituality that is naturally fluid and flexible and that allows freedom to conceptualise and articulate, without excessive modelling into types of master-slave relationships, then the prognosis for an easy working relationship between the lower and the higher mind, resulting in the effective and relaxed achievement of life goals, is considerably enhanced.

We have elected this particular individual partly on the basis that he experienced no indoctrination into rigid religious understanding. In that, the outcome has been effective.

CHAPTER TWENTY TWO

Interlude: Six

22 September

I've re-read the entry from 26 August on evoking the strong self. It helps explain my curious state of being unworried at progress, or lack of it, in addressing the task for which I came here. This afternoon I was very interested in solving my boredom problem – even though I had just completed an interesting and probably important transcript. So I enthusiastically jumped in the car to go the Kuaotunu for entertainment. I bought the *New Zealand Herald* in its new small format, and a peanut slab. Due to forswearing sugar, I have not had one of those in years, so that was a small celebration.

I sat on the beach edge under trees in the lee of the hill in the brilliant sun and got much hotter there than at Matapaua, read the paper and rested. And having taken respite, I happily came back and baked a cake.

Unfortunately, the mouse had been living in the stove, so instead of enjoying the cake smell as it cooked, the place soon stank of mouse urine again! But opening the doors and windows soon dispelled the bad smell. And the cake tasted okay. Tomorrow I'll dismantle the oven to clean it further. What a lot of impact one small rodent can have.

A really strange event occurred later on, waking after a nap. I felt something jumping around on the duvet near my right foot. It felt about the weight of a mouse. Thinking another rodent was with me, I kicked out, intending to send it to the floor. But there was no sound at all. And no further movement, even though I waited quietly. I then looked under the bed, but without result. I picked up my clothes carefully before dressing. There was no sign of insect or rodent.

The persistent impression I have is that the dead mouse returned in spirit to playfully recreate its happy presence in my awareness to relieve my sadness at causing its demise. Folly? Possibly. Or not. I may never know. But I have talked to several widows who have described their dead and buried partner leaving physical impressions on the bedding as they came present again in spirit to console their lover in her grief.

Later I went to Whitianga, where I bought two second-hand books, walked around to familiarise myself with the harbour area, and bought food at the one supermarket.

Back at home I munched a sandwich, then satisfied my escapist craving by reading a Catherine Cookson love story until one in the morning! Interestingly, the heroine's prime love object was a congenitally scarred man who had conversations with his higher self. Good choice.

23 September

09:14. Last night before sleeping I endeavoured to scan around me for perceptions related to an internal comment I heard about the cause of my antipathy towards continuing channelling yesterday being related to a demon. I saw no evidence of that, merely shapes similar to brown flax or seaweed moving as if in gentle currents of clear brown water on the sea bed. Strange. But no energy signature or hazard of any kind. More tests?

Of both perception and emotion. This process taxes your energy and patience. That is why the process is slow, to use your term. To us it is not slow, merely appropriate. It is without time limits such as you imagine apply. There are no time limits. Be at peace. Do your washing. Read your books and take pleasure in them. You are home here and need be nowhere else.

24 September

06:48. I was urged to not even make a drink before beginning this next series of questions. As is detailed below, I felt satisfied in all of my appetites. An unusual condition.

We have as our prerogative the capacity to enhance this individual's willingness and capacity to respond to impulses and communication through the link between the higher and the lower minds. It is our pleasure to do this, as well as our will. We have his cooperation due to a detailed understanding of the prerequisites of both the physical body and the lower mind to achieve a condition of willingness to accede to these requests.

We have now rested it by not demanding or requesting communication for two days. In that time it has entertained itself with discussions and described experiences in other places and other times in the form of two books.

Those excursions of the mind away from the conditions of the body, resting unobstructed as it feeds and nurtures itself in familiar ways with food, drink and entertainment of various kinds, including radio listening and reviewing this material on the laptop computer, has been sufficient to distribute its willingness through a variety of priorities and preferences in such a way that, at the level of ordinary existence, it feels satisfied. As a result, willingness returns to turn its attention to the discourse stimulated by the questions under review.

We understand these things. We would refer the reader to the ox-herding pictures from a far distant time in Daoist China. The intention then was to capture a representation of the difficulties involved in reconciling the drives inherent in the lower mind with the impulses perceived by the higher mind. Making that specific link, we draw attention to the venerable history associated with this realm of understanding human functioning. The choice now is to re-frame that ancient ox as the present obtuse lower mind and allocate the alert refined individual chasing the ox as the higher mind. This reversal of roles in relation to the ancient illustrations better matches this contemporary description.

We turn now to the the next questions.

CHAPTER TWENTY THREE

On Human Consciousness (Continued)

Q 90. What are the differences and similarities between thought in the embodied physical realm and thought in the spiritual realm? I am enquiring here about both the content and the quality of thought. You have previously stated that greater insights are possible in a disembodied state than in an embodied state because the observer is free of limiting physical sense perceptions. What other qualities are principally associated with disembodied spiritual thought?

We would say that thought in the higher mind is not intrinsically different from thought in the lower mind. However, there are impediments in the lower mind that do not exist within the higher mind.

In the lower mind there are multiple modes and interruptions that impact on the clear functioning of discursive thinking. In the higher mind information processing is more straightforward, less interrupted, and less interfered with. The body is a troublesome organism, in the sense that it has definite and inflexible requirements to maintain its condition through adequate nutrition and all that involves. There are no such impediments at the level of the higher mind.

Within the realm of existence we have modelled as agapéic space, the higher self is not beset with challenges in the sense of potential predators or radiations or compulsions from different orders of being. There is no social hierarchy to be manipulated or deferred to. There is only self-existence and the goal of self-optimisation.

There is also no time. Therefore the attention of the higher mind can be directed without interruption into any realm of existence or understanding that it chooses. When not required to attend to the lower mind and its associated organism, it is free to sustain relationships of its choosing and to enhance its understanding in any of many indescribable ways. Existence is a shockingly complex undertaking scarcely conceivable at the level of the lower mind.

The distinction between the two centres of conscious awareness is occasionally identifiable through activities such as this, whereby the clarity of mind, and the capacity to direct the attention for either short or long periods in a manner apparently independent of time, is neither more nor less than exactly that.

Accessing the higher mind's level of awareness is normally associated with apparent disruptions or discontinuities in the ordinary awareness of passing time. But that is a product and consequence of the functioning of bio-consciousness, not of Dao-consciousness.

Q 91. To what extent are we able to access the higher mind's thoughts while living in an embodied state?

We have just referred to the general consequence of accessing thoughts within the higher mind, noting its correlation with apparent disturbances in ordinary time-bound awareness. There are some preconditions and some consequences. The preconditions are well-known already, but we will repeat them for the purposes of answering the question fully.

The body must attain a condition of rest. Its biological necessities must be satisfied. Its basic requirements need to be relieved, and the prerequisites for good biological functioning met in advance, in order for there to be no component present that would introduce disharmony into the lower mind. With no appetite stimulated, and no need for sustenance or sleep, all these need to be satisfied, and to remain satisfied for a sufficient period of time that the lower mind's attention may be successfully directed in a sustained fashion in a manner of its choosing.

It may also choose, as in these present conditions, to attend to input not merely from within its own level of discursive thought, but to information on offer through the link between it and the higher mind. If active dialogue is indulged in, or even entertainment sought by way of imagery or imagination from the level of the higher mind, then these can be engaged in. Further, if there is serious purpose, and a sustained practice for attending to the deep questions of existence, as in this case, then explicit support is available. There is a willingness to bring all avenues of support from the level of the higher mind, and beyond. For this is what becomes necessary in conducting that class of enquiry.

The resources of the higher mind are substantial, yet limited. On those occasions when the lower mind manifests a serious intent to investigate a particular domain of existence and experience, or an accumulated history and its affiliated understanding, and that enquiry necessarily involves resources at the mental level beyond even those of the particular higher mind associated with the individual lower mind raising these issues, then all resources are able to be brought to bear in a complete manner so as to conduct a disciplined recounting of any and all factors relevant to the enquiry.

And so it is in this case. There has been, sustained now for hundreds of centuries as measured in local time, a willingness to nurture the valuable investment of spiritual resources into a process deemed part of this large experiment. Those are the things which are available for access.

Q 92. What are the differences and similarities between emotion in the embodied physical realm and emotions in the spiritual realm?

Animal passions, the biological drives associated with food, sex, territory, survival and reproduction, and socially conditioned behaviours and identity, collectively constitute and dominate the emotions we experience in our everyday embodied states. I assume emotions associated with the spiritual sphere are oriented around agapé and include such emotions as compassion, self-sacrifice and nurturing others. So:

(a) How do these spiritual emotions impact in our embodied existence?

(b) What should we be doing with them?

Part (a) implies the existence of emotion at the spiritual level, and that distinction may be made between emotion at the level of the biological organism and of the higher mind.

It is perfectly true. This has been the subject of substantial investigation throughout time. Classes of thought and classes of feeling may be distinguished. A convenient way of mapping these distinctions has been by associating them with different levels of functioning. We assert that this continues to be appropriate.

The function of the higher mind is to convey, process and manifest qualities of thought and feeling. This describes particular aspects of thought within the higher mind itself that exist in a pattern able to be communicated to any associated physical organisms in such a way as to influence their preferences.

So-called finer feelings are experienced, and manifest in that manner, precisely because they reside and originate at a different level. We explicitly identify that level as being within the higher mind. We firmly co-associate it with the model of agapéic space, this being a model of existence that describes the phenomenon of the human being throughout its various levels of existence.

How such thoughts and finer feelings impact on the level of embodied human existence is determined partially by the local identity, that is, by the bio-conscious awareness functioning at the level of the lower mind.

Where a pattern of understanding is pre-inculcated into an individual's lower mind, that is, by a system of educational understanding and valuing and preference, the self-aware individual has the capacity, at any moment, to receive input from the higher mind. Knowing the nature of the input, the lower mind may address it and render it preferentially in a way that enables it to attend to the bio-consciousness and its drives and modes of functioning, while simultaneously remaining alert and responsive to those categories of input from the higher mind.

What that alert responsiveness has the potential to do is to shift the habitual locus of awareness from being contained only within the lower mind and its necessary functions, and to move it some way towards greater involvement in, awareness of, and input from the thoughts and feelings associated with the higher mind. To the extent that such a preferred nature is successfully inculcated into the functioning organism at the bio-consciousness level, then particular higher qualities of character result.

Accordingly, there are ranges of opportunity. They extend from a quality of personality and preference solely and exclusively focussed on the bio-consciousness and its modes of awareness, with zero input from the higher mind and zero knowledge of or willingness to attend to that level of input, to something approaching a hundred percent attendance to the conversational mode associated with the connection between the lower and higher minds.

The issue here is to establish a flexible and attentive bio-conscious awareness that may be interrupted from any level of need. If the life plan requires it, there may be constructed an alert, responsive and attentive individual capable of responding to input from any level, because it knows the range of options. If that is done, and we acknowledge that, in fact, it is applicable only to a small subset of humanity, then a higher order of functioning is possible.

If is not done, or if it is done partially, then what is structured into existence is an alert and attentive individual with anything from zero to minor willingness, capacity or understanding to attend to the subconscious level of input available from the higher mind. It may never be brought to the level of conscious awareness within the individual's entire lifetime. And that may be completely appropriate and adequate for the life plan involved.

We here introduce the idea that awareness of the input from the higher mind, and communication with it, is not a necessity for all individuals. Very commonly it is required by only a small number, or by a small percentage, of any population. Many or most individuals living out their life in their elected body, attending to the variety of relationships involved in living a satisfying life, can be entirely and properly content doing so.

This is not to say that they may not benefit from awareness of such higher level communicative possibilities within themselves. But they do not require it. Therefore for them to be made guilty to any degree for their apparent incapacity to access those realms is entirely inappropriate.

Those who spontaneously manifest those qualities of attending to input from the higher mind are best encouraged to do exactly that. And those whose prime purpose is to manifest input from those levels are best supported in their desire and capacity to involve themselves in it. For all is choice. No person is intrinsically wrong in these matters.

(b) What should we be doing with these spiritual emotions? To the extent that they manifest, attend to them. Otherwise they are wasted.

Q 93. We often fail to make the most of opportunities presented to us. Negative emotions, unprocessed trauma, and self-limiting and self-destructive habitual behaviours limit our perceptions, hinder our ability to process the information we receive, and lead us to act in ways that we later wish we hadn't.

Your comments on dealing with blockages and limiting factors?

An individual may be optimally characterised as completely implementing the process of taking a body, developing it, and living a life such that it comes to a successful conclusion.

In relation to this, there is a scale of possible outcomes that result from an excursion into a life that naturally ranges from sub-optimal, to optimal, to ecstatic. Within this range an individual's manifest qualities encompass unlimited possibilities, given that self-optimisation potentially leads to the individual accessing ecstatic states.

Where an individual grows up in a subculture that inculcates a clear awareness of manifesting optimal rather than sub-optimal states, opportunities are freely available for attending to various trauma and for dealing with their impact on the emotions and psyche in such a way as to clear them from impacting further on the developing organism. The result is that the individual's capacity to optimally process physical, emotional and spiritual input is enhanced.

Where an individual grows up in an environment in which none of those processes are available, then it simply makes its path as best it can, through its intrinsic capacities to manifest what in that subculture would be perceived as either erotic or ecstatic states, which are categorised by such a subculture as the unfamiliar, or the wrong, or the crazy.

It is possible to categorise entire civilisations, or sub-components of each civilisation, as constituting an environment that, in terms of supporting the life of its citizens so they develop into optimal forms, as inadequate, adequate or better than adequate. However, it is also the case that almost any civilisation contains within itself a vast range of opportunities for individuals to find their place within it in a way that is congruent with their life plan. Civilisations are that complex in their organisation.

This implies that a monoculture imposed by an authoritarian ruler is not optimal. A condition whereby a culture is subservient to some external culture is also not optimal. What is optimal is a condition whereby an individual is free, within any existing culture, to sample every apparently relevant quality of input from the range of opportunities that surround it, in such a way that it has freedom of choice in association with a degree of awareness of its pre-life plan.

Living in an optimal sub-component of such a civilisation, every individual is briefly informed of the range of options for its life. It is not blamed if it chooses any one or other class of activity and associated education. But it is informed that the range of possibilities are wide and that it has the capacity to choose. Choosing can include requests for further information, if the individual elects to enquire.

And so the development of every individual living in such an optimal culture is allowed, to a degree and in a direction congruent with its life plan. It is free to develop sets and qualities of relationships in such a manner as to lead it, by the conclusion of its life, to the perception that it had purpose in associating with humanity, and that humanity had supported it in its development and enquiry, insofar as that by its life's end it had been able to sample those chosen activities and modes of functioning in a way that pleased it and satisfied its life plan.

For the ordinary individual growing up in a modern culture there are endless opportunities for making optimal choices and sub-optimal choices. Neither are wrong. But they bring consequences. And it is through such consequences, and through the impact of those consequences on others around them, that rich karma may be generated, along with the reduction of karma.

In a free society, all of these activities constitute grist for the mill of the node of Dao-consciousness to manifest its intentions. And properly so.

25 September

Q 94. We learn and develop through repetition. We learn to talk by repeating what others say to us. Practice enables us to become better at any task. Through repeated application we transform weaknesses into strengths and abilities into skills. Repetition is key to our development as human beings.

The same process clearly applies to our growth as spiritual nodes of consciousness. We are repeatedly incarnated into bodies so that, through repetition, we learn to do living as best we can. Your comments on the need for repetition in an experiential sense?

Coming as we do from a place where the repetition referred to in this question has been the subject of our direct experience, but at a level more general than what is referred to in this case, we can affirm that the repetition of multiple life times is indeed necessary to transmit the breadth of encountered information.

This includes what to do with that information, how to treat it, how to combine it, how to categorise it, how to see relevance between sets of information, and how to partition information so as to order it, stack it, style it and make it comprehensible.

The task of the reincarnating node of Dao-consciousness is to reflect, at the end of each incarnation, in order to do exactly those things. The capacity to consider the ordering of information, to perceive at the level of the conscious mind categories of metaphors, their relationship, and their status as nested one into the other in the manner of a file in a folder, is essential in order to compact the information into personally derived categories of storage.

It is our task to extend those metaphors and processes into a hierarchical ordered system in order for the model of incarnation to become useful within the context of this metaphor, itself a description of the process that it is part of. We will begin with the fundamentals, and then attempt to extend them in logical order. So:

Any event encountered in a life already comprises multiple categories of potential classification. The naive node of Dao-consciousness has little experience of registering, let alone ordering, such categories of information into its own personal set of files. It is the process of recognising, categorising, ordering and filing these classes of information that constitutes a necessary process, not only within the bio-consciousness, but also within the Dao-consciousness. This is a little-recognised necessity.

The ordering of life experience within the Dao-consciousness is what enables it to analyse and interpret the information it encounters, using the resources at its disposal, which usually consists of the bio-consciousness of the awake and alert human mind. When information is both interpretable and interpreted, it forms an instantaneous reference set of categories that is available to use to make predictions based on prior experience. Events are continuously classified as they unfold.

The distinction between a naive and an experienced individual, in terms of their experience during incarnation, is that an experienced individual will keep ahead of unfolding of events through the process of having already recognised, classified, analysed and made predictions from them. And not just simple predictions, but complex predictions. Accordingly, they recognise that of the range of potential outcomes they face, only some are relevant and probable. So it is the development of their capacity to analyse events, and to predict their trajectory, which leads such individuals to be recognised as experienced practitioners of the art of incarnation. Because they have already encountered much and processed very large quantities of the resulting information.

This is the necessary practice of an individual node of Dao-consciousness, not only during incarnation, but also subsequent to it. The process of analysing and reflecting on a just-completed life forms the work of the node of Dao-consciousness subsequent to each exploration of physicality. That analysis enables the node to recognise patterns of incomplete understanding and knowledge, and to survey categories of experience that may be potentially useful in another incarnation. It then selects from those categories in order to encounter them in its next incarnation. From this analysis the next life plan is created. And we have previously expounded at some length on life plans.

Accordingly, the practice of repeated incarnation is the superficial activity. Behind it much analysis necessarily occurs, both within incarnation and out of it, as we have said. It is an ongoing instantaneous process, as well as a reflective process, carried out at each significant event, wringing from it all it contains by way of implication and probability.

Not recognised in the scientistic world view, because of its short-sighted understanding, is a range of activity for which the bio-consciousness is a required article. This activity includes the process of instantaneous analysis that is ongoing each moment during an activity, creating predictions of probabilities for the next few moments in order to properly guide the bio-consciousness on its path through its day, and especially through social interactions.

Here we venture into what many would consider speculative or ungrounded statements. But we say that part of the reason for the necessary increase in the human animal's cranial capacity was to accommodate a more complex brain, such that a more sophisticated, alert and aware mind could capture and process a greater order of magnitude of information that was potentially at hand as a result of incarnation into physicality, and to analyse it at a suitable rate.

This is the implication. The necessary corollary of incarnation is the quantities of information being traded, as it were. They are mind-bogglingly huge. Most individuals do not comprehend the depth of analysis that accompanies and drives every daily activity not comprising a habituated action. But this is the result for which incarnation is undertaken.

This is the promise and the possibility of incarnation, which every node of Dao-consciousness willingly dives into physicality to obtain. It is the gold, the nugget, the pearl beyond price, to use those common metaphors.

Q 95. You have stated that as a node we each carry an agapé component and a hierarchy component. They are acquired in the sense that as we develop we raise the level of our personal agapé and hierarchy components, or we rise in relation to them. I have four questions about this. (a) What is your definition of agapé?

Our definition of agapé is that it is the nature intrinsic to Dao-consciousness. Loving regard, a desire to help, wishing the best for any other, self-concentration into goodness, willingness to love all others, and a desire to rise on the morrow in a bright new day, also described as an optimistic and positive outlook, are all part of it.

This definition of agapé has been given in other places. But we would extend on it now in response to this information by claiming some additional components.

The desire to nurture is part of it. The willingness to focus on any individual is part of it, so it is not self-interested but other-interested. The capacity to hold a group in special relationship is part of it. A willingness to see beyond the superficial personality to the core of another person's nature is part of it. Recognising that any other is intrinsically and at core identical to oneself is part of it. And claiming commonality with all others, human and non-human, is part of it.

Q 95. (b) What is your definition of hierarchy?

Hierarchy is the attribute which constitutes the sum and product of loving acts throughout a life. It can only be added up at the end of a life, which is the reason why movement in hierarchy is most often assigned at the end of an incarnation.

Unusual or rare individuals conduct themselves within a life in such a manner as to earn, by virtue of significant acts, the opportunity to make an advance in hierarchy during a life rather than at the life's end. The extent of the hierarchy scale has never been discussed in detail. We will take the opportunity to do so.

A nominal designation would comprise one hundred steps. Each step is necessarily subdivided in order to accommodate the opportunity for a manifest increase in hierarchy status due to advancing within each of a thousand lifetimes. But to subdivide it more finely would provide excessive exactitude that is not useful to individual aspirants. So we will not do that. We will designate one hundred as a ramp or scale, literally a ladder of advancement. Jacob's Ladder and other similar ladder-like metaphors indicate the scale of hierarchy.

The number of steps comprising one hundred allows any individual to apply the common percentage scale and so easily visualise it for themselves, for example through using the scale of value comprising money. To have reached the value of a whole dollar, or any other similar designated unit in a cash transaction, is to anchor the concept of hierarchy in the familiar, specifically in relation to value.

One difficulty of working with a multi-axial space such as agapéic space arises because it comprises three dimensions that necessarily contain fundamentally different attributes. So the position of any individual within agapéic space is only partially determined by the scale of hierarchy.

It is certainly true that the scale of hierarchy represents the encountering of much experience, the processing of much experience, the assigning of value to that experience, and the reformulation of the nature of the individual as a consequence.

Therefore it is entirely appropriate to imagine that a naive node of Dao-consciousness has a hierarchy of one. Not zero, but one. From that it can be appreciated that there exists an incremental scale by which individuals can be assessed, using both self-assessment and other-assessment, with respect to their willingness to offer loving acts, based on their understanding of having done so in the past. We refer here to understanding derived from processing the resultant information.

The metaphor is approximate, of course. It is indicative. In fact, in most instances it is of small utility. And yet it offers a clear indication that there is a product and consequence in the benefit and desirability of acting in a loving manner.

Q 95. (c) What do agapé and hierarchy correspond to within our consciousness?

The will to act from agapé produces hierarchy, and we mean that in an incremental sense. Utilising the just given components of our definition of agapé, it becomes possible to map those components of awareness within which the products of agapé and hierarchy may reside, the tendencies which support them, and the tendencies which negate them. However, we will not specify such things.

Partly, this is because it is a complex undertaking. Partly it is because the product of a life is to form precisely these connections between attitude, act and outcome. And partly it is because it is what every individual comes into physicality for. It constitutes the work of incarnation, which is to so master these things as to eventually confidently know and act as what is identified as an individual of uncompromising goodwill.

So we will not specify what this question asks for.

Q 95. (d) As we develop, how does our position change in relation to agapé and hierarchy?

The metaphor of agapéic space comprises a navigable space. Generally speaking, an individual initially comes into a position within that space corresponding to low hierarchy, low willingness to bequest agapé, and minimal agapéic frequency. This is its initial band of occupancy on that scale. It progresses incrementally in terms of hierarchy, agapéic frequency and willingness to bequest agapé. The end point is at the normal position of exit from the human zone of occupancy. We have already specified this zone to be from twenty-five to thirty-five in agapéic frequency, without breaking that down into its finest divisions.

This comprises a probabilistic trajectory. No individual trajectory can be predicted precisely, because the exact trajectory is a consequence of the working out of the sum of all lives for any individual.

In that sense, a person is not the same person. Speaking in terms of the person as the node of Dao-consciousness, at the end of its trajectory the node is not the same as it was at the beginning. It is a graduation in a literal as well as a metaphorical sense. We will not describe the zone of occupancy beyond the point of graduation, because it is not our brief.

CHAPTER TWENTY-FOUR

On Reincarnation

Q 96. What is the mathematics of reincarnation? The Earth's human population has increased exponentially over the last one hundred years. Either:

(a) Many new human spiritual identities have been created to "fill" the vastly greater number of available bodies, or:

(b) Individual spiritual identities previously reincarnated with large gaps between incarnations, and now there is little gap, or:

(c) Spiritual identities from elsewhere in the universe are entering human bodies to make up the numbers.

What is your response to these three options?

We would respond to this question and its options in the following ways.

The opportunity that this planet represents is for occupancy of one or two species for the purpose of acquiring incarnational experience in order to advance the trajectory of understanding of a corresponding node of Dao-consciousness. There is no shortage of nodes of Dao-consciousness. This planet is just one of an essentially unlimited number of locations in which a node of Dao-consciousness can elect to endure an incarnation.

Although we have said that it is not common for an individual node of Dao-consciousness to cross species, there are some who do. However, the shared existence of a node of Dao-consciousness is in no way limited by the population of this planet. It never will be. In this small corner of this universe, this planet is just one of an essentially unlimited range of opportunities to encounter physicality and learn as a result.

The degree to which this question is predicated on ideas of limitation is inescapable. The difficulty is in the limited capacity to recognise the true magnitude and complexity of the physical universe, and even then only this one. What is also not recognised is the fountain of available nodes of Dao-consciousness, and not only of the magnitude suitable for assignment to this particular species. The prolific nature of the Dao is completely unrecognised as a premise in this question.

There is and never will be any lack of individuals willing to take residence in the physicality associated with this particular planet, let alone all others. With that we render the question, and its premise, inapplicable.

Q 97. What is the average number of incarnations? In Agapé and the Hierarchy of Love *you suggest one thousand. I think you also stated that Buddha took around 360 incarnations. What is the average range of incarnations?*

We have given the average range of incarnations in terms of the model that we are presenting to be on average one thousand, but subject to two standard deviations less than that and over five standard deviations more than one thousand. The number of incarnations of Gautama Buddha comprised 513, not 360.

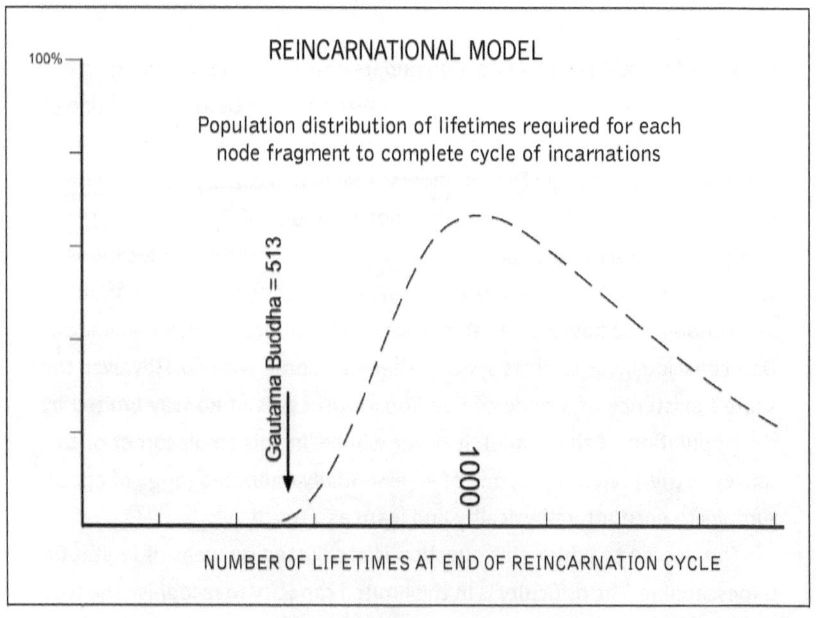

FIGURE 24.1

Q 98. Spiritual traditions maintain that the goal of spirituality is to escape from the rounds of births and deaths. Being caught up in the rounds of births and deaths is seen as spiritually limiting, even negative, while escaping the rounds of births and deaths is the pinnacle of earthly spiritual achievement.

In religions such as Christianity and Islam, where reincarnation is not taught, the idea is instead that certain people are saved and others are not, due to what they believe and do.

Clearly, your concept of spirituality does not include the idea that some people are saved and others are condemned. Neither does it include the idea that being incarnated into a body is a spiritually bad thing. Instead, you view incarnation as a spiritual good that facilitates our growth.

So you are actually presenting a new spiritual paradigm in relation to the purpose of incarnating over an extended series of lives. Please clarify this change in perspective and the paradigm change that underlies it.

The premise behind Question 98 is that descriptions of spirituality maintain their validity of over long periods of time. That is not the case.

Each new generation requires more individuals to articulate their personal perspective and reflections according to their understanding and their indoctrination. Where documents exist to bring a sense of stability to such perspectives, there are even more individuals willing to interpret, to reinterpret the interpretation, and to reinterpret the interpretation of the interpretation. So the opportunity for error increases, not decreases. And that is within only one language and a few generations.

Understanding this well, spiritual traditions attempt to enclose documentation into few copies, or into authorised sub-copies. Even that is insufficient to contain the willingness of poorly educated individuals to speculate without limit, and even, over a period of time, to reverse meanings of the terminology associated with the original texts.

We take the example of the virgin birth, a clearly nonsensical claim which has been given its status precisely because of its improbability. Yet in the original terminology we understand the term virgin to have meant first. A first-born. Nothing to do with spiritual impregnation.

Yet we grant the congruence between those two concepts is not entirely inappropriate, for it is true that the many individuals for whom virgin birth has been claimed are a product of a spiritual impregnation. And thus the term has encoded an awareness of the gestation of an individual derived from spiritual existence, not from physicality.

The collection and history of metaphors associated with descriptions of spirituality have accumulated into many traditions. Changes in sets of metaphors has meant that confusion increases, not decreases, over time.

We can do nothing about this. But it is in recognition of exactly that fact that we bring again into this period of time, and into this particular language, an opportunity to refresh understanding in order to acquaint the currently existing population, and future populations, to the extent that they elect to find it, that a coherent description has been brought present once again.

Q 99. What is the criteria according to which we no longer need to reincarnate and can go on to the next stage? Presumably, in a general sense we can say that it is the result of sufficient development and maturity.

(a) What are the criteria by which development and maturity may be measured, by which the cycle of reincarnation comes to an end?

(b) Is being aware we are an embodied node part of that process?

We have already stated that the criteria (which must be exceeded) by which a series of incarnations comes to an end is nothing other than the resolute determination to act from agapé no matter what the consequences to the organism an individual is embodied within.

There is a criteria which involves an individual node being examined and consequently graduating. So the series of incarnations concludes with the node's graduation. We have already stated that those at higher levels will not tolerate contrary custom. The graduation itself is a consequence of the degree to which the individual is resolutely determined to act in a way congruent with spiritual values and aspirations, and this determination takes precedence in every situation, whether speculative or real.

Graduation is a consequence of evaluation made by individuals who possess higher hierarchy and greater, or even grander, willingness to bequest agapé. They are at least partially reintegrated identities who have largely completed the process of integrating their full round of lifetimes of experience, by which they have qualified themselves for the role of examiner of any aspirant seeking to conclude their round of incarnations.

It is not an exaggeration to say that there are close examinations that infiltrate into the aspirant's attributes. There is no means by which premature graduation from the class of incarnating individuals can be achieved. The examination is thorough and theoretically without end.

The individual who succeeds in that examination can be relied on to willingly confront every aspect of their experience, and to categorise, sort and integrate it even more than they have already done.

They will also be willing to meet all those other individuals who comprise fragments of the original undivided node of Dao-consciousness in such a way that they abrade away every distinction. They achieve this by processing every element of every experience in every incarnation across the entire group of approximately a thousand individuals. They come to know each other at each level of their experiential understanding and existence that they joyfully merge with them, whether one by one or in groups, in such a manner that they lose their individuality and to see themselves as so intrinsically similar that they combine with no distinction between them.

It is that prospect, as much as anything else, that they should so love their brother, meaning the other fragments of the originating node of Dao-consciousness, that they are willing to lose their entire sense of separate identity and to see their unity as a natural outcome, proper and complete to every detail.

It is only when an individual so values the associated values and trappings of a response to life from agapé, from agapé and nothing else, that they qualify themselves to elude the grasp of the physical.

For this crucible of life, this process of repeated incarnation, is such as to mould an individual, to create them in diverse ways from diverse sources, and to render them indistinguishable from one another. To accrete and accrete difference, then to abrade and abrade difference, grinding so finely as to polish the pearl of great price into the lustrous wonder that results.

These excursions into metaphor are deliberate. The capacity of the ordinary individual to deal with the massive complexity of analysis of the multiple layers compounded from each set of information, acquired during the course of each incarnation, is such as to make it impossible to encode all that is involved within ordinary language.

Thus we use the metaphors of value, of preciousness, of intrinsic beauty, which are embodied in the idea of a gem valued for its capacity to reflect and refract light. Hence its shine and polish. And hence it may be characterised as being "a cut above", in the sense of being cut "from above" by a master of the art of the creation of unflawed beauty. These are metaphors to render conceivable to the ordinary mind what is otherwise inconceivable.

And so the metaphors of the unflawed gem, the pearl of great price gleaming in unearthly light, are suitable constructs by which to establish, in the mind of any person considering these things, that there are parameters, and degrees on such parameters, and scales of height, which one can only dream of aspiring to within an ordinary life. But they indicate it is possible to eventually come into an unearthly condition. And this is true.

These metaphors have accumulated around every tradition of spiritual understanding worthy of the name. But the ordinary individual, focused on ordinary life and its exigencies, necessities, compulsions and attractions, is obviously so far removed from those qualities as to lead some to despair of reaching that state within a lifetime.

It is entirely true that that is generally impossible. But as a long-term goal, which is aspired to only in the relatively advanced stages of a round of incarnations, and which is earnestly worked for, then embraced in relaxed understanding, it is valid, worthy, and to be pursued.

These, then, are the criteria by which individuals advance beyond their last incarnation into a state of existence which cannot be described using these metaphors.

In answer to (b), it is unquestionably true that being aware of being an embodied spiritual being is part of the process of moving beyond that.

Q 100. Do all embodied individuals realise they are a spiritually embodied being and remember past lives before they stop incarnating?

To graduate from their series of incarnations, individuals must understand themselves in detail, down to the level of every significant action in every significant life. It is also necessary to recall the fact of prior incarnations, and be able to articulate this recall within the conscious mind at the level of bio-conscious awareness.

Such information may be used in a variety of ways. Or it can be hidden from others. The usual criteria of personality apply, except an individual near mastery, recalling lifetimes of experience, also possesses the capacity to evaluate the utility of broadcasting that fact.

In many instances the qualities of character developed by that stage are such as to recognise there is no utility in advertising the fact. So such individuals, even though they thoroughly understand their circumstance and condition, including their personal history through many lifetimes, if not yet all, are entirely willing to hide their understanding from almost every other individual incarnated identity.

For what is the value of doing so? To advertise themselves as being a madman, if that is the nature of the culture into which they are incarcerated? To proclaim themselves in an egotistical manner so that they attain positions of high degree? If that were the case, they would not be who they claim to be. Because they would thoroughly understand by that stage that any individual, egotistically making such claims, is exactly other than their claim to be an individual of perspicacity and internal value.

Accordingly, we are willing to state that an individual who makes such claims in an overt public way is unlikely to be an individual near the term of their series of incarnations. The individual generally decreed by those who know them as having unrevealed depths, while yet obviously embodying competence, is a more likely candidate for identification as an individual experienced in the incarnatory process.

So the answer to the question is yes.

* * * * *

With that, we conclude. We declare this set of questions complete and answered in every relevant detail.

There are many other elements we could respond to. Expansions could be made and implications refined. However, we do not recommend that be done to their limit, or anywhere near it, for this is intended to be a general model, not a complete model mapped to every detail.

We congratulate the individuals involved for their diligence, cooperation and willingness to assist us and each other in this nontrivial task of bringing such a model-set before the public eye.

The book will not sell well, of course. But it will take its place among a growing number of others that, in due time, have the capacity to modulate individuals' understanding and their willingness to place themselves within a larger set of parameters than they may have been inculcated into during the course of their education.

This book will be joined by others over time. There will be many differences between these new model-sets. And those individuals who seek to investigate them will find much joy in refining the differences or finding commonalities, a task that has occupied innumerable individuals across time and cultures.

Accordingly, this is merely a contribution by which to trigger further analysis, consideration and understanding of the role of the individual as a fragment of a node of Dao-consciousness, to use our preferred terminology, as it strives to find its place within this particular world and to change itself.

The pearl of great price is worthy of every endeavour. And we bless those who seek it.

CHAPTER TWENTY-FIVE

Postscript

At various times we have become aware of opportunities to contribute to humanity's perception of their place in the world.

Those who have fallen into physicality, asleep and unaware of their origins and of their capacity to investigate those origins in such ways as these, have stimulated us to contribute to their awaking and understanding. That process is largely complete at this point. We anticipate little need to again provide such detailed explanatory metaphors as have been provided here. Therefore, it is unreasonable to expect any large-scale expansion on this model-set. In our estimation, this is sufficient.

Having provided the primary literature, it is now the work of the progenitors of secondary literature to expand on this missive to humanity in whatever ways they choose. Certainly, there are many possibilities. Pre-existing models may provide the basis for some such analysis. We prognosticate they are likely to arise in due course.

But that is not our purpose. It is not our role. We will likely decline to contribute to the generation of secondary-level literature. That is not to say that we will be unaware of it. Just that we see our role in its evocation as having been completed. Nor is that to say we will remain unaware of, or unresponsive to, individuals who aspire after these same processes in order to enrich their own incarnated lives, or series of lives, in order to add to their personal well-being, understanding, personal development, and to their capacity to contribute to humanity as a whole.

Therefore this should not be viewed as a one-off event of intrusion into physicality carried out for a particular purpose. Instead, it is merely one of a series of such intrusions, carried out in such a manner as to contribute in the ways we have said.

It is also possible for individuals to focus their awareness and intention and attempt to communicate with not only this particular reunited and re-integrated identity nearing the end of its unification process, but also with other reintegrated identities. Because, of course, there are many others. We would speak briefly to that.

In the past we have specified that every complete node of Dao-consciousness supervises, if one could think of it that way, approximately one third of their number. And hence has been generated the historical awareness of the roles of many gods, as they have traditionally been identified.

We prefer to use different language here, for god-language too easily generates a master-slave relationship, which we reject because it lacks utility. Nevertheless, it is true that while we ourselves elect to contribute in this way to the requests of humanity, to answer their prayers (to use god-language), and to facilitate their progress (to use less linguistically determined language), we affirm that there are many others, in or near our condition, whose intention it is similarly to reach back into humanity and contribute to the quality and meaning of human lives.

So we come among you. As do many others. This is the means by which there have come to be the many records now in existence of pronouncements generated by one identity or another, named or unnamed, all with the aim of bringing to humanity a category of literature by which to inspire those who encounter it.

This transmission is no different. Therefore we claim no special place for it in that genre of literature. It is just another example, another sample, of a category of proposed understanding brought into the human world because they ask for it, and indeed have done so throughout time. And there is no greater need now than at any other time. In fact, quite the reverse could be argued.

So as a summary and codicil to this small item of literature, we close by saying that for every individual who encounters these things there will be at least ten others who do not. And there is nothing wrong with that. Therefore the urge to proselytise must be firmly restrained.

Of course, the urge to investigate is a curiosity-driven enterprise that aims at encountering all that the human world can provide and bringing understanding to the individual. It is a joyful undertaking. We wish each individual joy in this task.

Glossary

Agapé: From the Greek, meaning selfless love. The word was adopted by Christian theologians to describe non-physical, spiritual love. Agapé is the nature intrinsic to Dao-consciousness.

Agapé frequency: One of three fundamental axes that define agapéic space. It has a scale comprising a nominal range of 0 – 65,000 discrete realms.

Agapéic space: A model and metaphor generated to describe spiritual existence. Agapéic space is defined by three axes at right angles to one another, these being agapéic frequency, hierarchy and willingness to bequest agapé. Agapéic space comprises the totality of existence, including the physical, astral and clear light domains. *See Air-fog model (in the Index)*.

Ask (of spirit): Spiritual identities commonly only communicate with human beings as a result of being asked. This enables them to avoid revoking any individual human being's free will.

Aura: The formative structure in the implicate order which partially defines the human physical body.

Avatar: An ancient Sanskrit word that refers to deity descending to the human realm and taking on a body. Krishna was reputedly an avatar of Vishnu. Recently the term avatar has been re-deployed to describe an identity virtually present in cyberspace or virtual reality. In the de-mythologised context transmitted in this book avatar is used to describe a perceptive individual whose life purpose is to establish a cooperative agreement with a node of Dao-consciousness of level significantly higher than 35 on the agape scale, then to investigate spiritual matters and communicate to others what is discovered.

Awareness: A state of elementary or undifferentiated consciousness.

Coalesence, co-association: The process by which an individual spiritual identity unites with, and animates, a human body.

Channel: A human being who serves as the medium for transmission, facilitating the movement of information from the spiritual to the physical domain and visa versa.

Clear light: Spiritual space perceived beyond the dim astral level. Experiences of this domain have been placed on the historical record by mystics.

Consciousness: Consciousness comes from, and is a node of, Dao. It functions on two levels, Dao-consciousness and bio-consciousness.

Dantian (tan tien): Chinese for bodily energy centres. Chakra is the more commonly used Indian term. Dantian is used in two senses:: (1) to refer to a node in interaction between the Dao-consciousness (spirit-form) and the auric layer of the human physical body, and (2) to the "kernel" at the centre of an individual spirit-sphere. *See Identity (spiritual)*.

Dao (Tao): The ultimate source of all that exists. Ultimate consciousness.

Emergence: On the cosmic level, emergence is a feature of the expansionary cycle of each universe. On the biological level, emergence is a process whereby life as a whole develops from lesser to greater complexity. Biologically, this also applies to species. On the spiritual level, emergence is a process whereby nodes manifest from the Dao.

Empirical: Based on, concerned with, or verified by using sense-based observation or experience, as opposed to theory or pure logic.

Energy (particle): An electrophysical phenomenon measured in electron volts.

Energy (physical): The capacity to do work.

Energy signature (spiritual): A complex array of information encoded within the aura that conveys all of an identity's characteristics. Perception of an energy signature enables the perceiver to assess another's character and trustworthiness, and hence to evaluate the risk of interacting.

Expansionary impulse: A fundamental undefined cosmic phenomenon, causally attributed as a motive for species emergence, development and conclusion.

Group soul: See *Soul*.

Hara: Japanese for belly. It is a dantian (energy centre) located approximately two finger-widths below the navel. As such, it is a patterning on the electrospiritual level derived from the implicate order. It is also the level on which the spirit-sphere manifests, and so may be interpreted as the level of actual human spiritual existence.

Haric space: Loosely used as an alternative name for agapéic space.

Hierarchy (social): A system or organization in which people are ranked above or below one another according to status or authority.

Hierarchy (spiritual): The attribute which constitutes the sum and product of loving acts throughout a life as one builds on one's history in other lifetimes.

Higher mind: A function of the higher self that processes spiritual information and manifests intellect and purpose. It is also where lower mind personality characteristics generated during incarnation are uploaded to and where those characteristics accumulate.

Higher mind's purpose: This is to integrate all gathered information, distil out repetition and redundancy, and come to clear mastery of everything associated with, related to, and implied by the accumulated information.

Higher self: The spiritual identity. It communicates with the lower self (that being the physical body and its brain) via the auric channel.

Human (conventional meaning): An individual consisting of body, social identity, mind and purpose.

Human (spiritual meaning): A spiritual identity who is either embodied or disembodied, and without reference to intended species of physical embodiment.

Humanity: The entire set of humans currently embodied.

Humanity (steady-state model): This transmission proposes that an endless and continuous stream of spiritual identity is cast from the Dao, some of which elects to mature and become refined by engaging in a process of repeated incarnation within the crucible offered by human existence on this planet. This process is beyond the comprehension of the human mind, and so cannot be defined by, or limited to, the human concepts of past or future. This renders meaningless all issues concerning end-times and related eschatological phenomena.

Identity (spiritual): Modelled as an essentially invisible sphere with a small kernel at its centre. It exists as a structure in agapéic space where it is able to move at will, but to a degree dependent on its spiritual development.

Implicate order: A subtle underlying component of reality proposed by physicist David Bohm. Here identified as the auric level structure necessarily associated with any living organism.

Individual (social): A single human being separate and distinct from others.

Individual (spiritual): A node of Dao-consciousness.

Intellect: That aspect of mind which processes information.

Intention: That process of mind which elects, evaluates and subsequently intends a specific outcome.

Karma: The outcome of human reactions which result in others being radically disempowered, confined or killed.

Keruru: The Maori name for a species of bird called wood-pigeon in English.

Light (physical): Electromagnetic radiation to which the human eye is sensitive, nominally of wavelength 380-720nm.

Light (spiritual): A subtle perception of brightness derived via the auric perceptual channel. Generally correlated with agapéic frequency, that is, dim at lower frequency and brighter at higher frequency levels.

Lingering spirit: A discarnate human identity which has not yet returned to the clear light, but remains in spiritual proximity to, and with its attention focussed on, embodied physical reality.

Lower mind: A function of the biological brain, it processes information and manifests habitual emotional characteristics that result from imprinting and enculturation.

Mind: *See Higher mind* and *Lower mind.*

Mingimingi: A Māori word meaning twisted. The name is used to describe at least two different species of New Zealand plants: *leucopogon fasciculatus*, a forest shrub, and *coprosma propinqua*, a widespread small leaved shrub.

Model: A hypothetical description of a complex entity or process. A representation of something, sometimes on a smaller scale.

Myth: A traditional story that recounts natural or historical events, often involving supernatural characters. Many religious myths are accepted by believers as historically true and as providing explanations for a people's worldview.

Node: A zone of concentration of some attribute.

Node of Dao-consciousness: A condition of concentrated consciousness within the unmanifest absolute that contains intellect and purpose.

observer: A large-scale emergent node of Dao-consciousness containing intellect and purpose. The unobserved initiator of the multiverse.

Outlier: A data point on the periphery of a data-set.

Point of attention: A product of focussed awareness, free to move without limit of space or time.

Purpose: See *Higher mind's purpose.*

Querent (group context): A participant in prospecting for experiential learning. One who takes part in the group with the explicit expectation that through group activities information useful to living may be gained. One who is present with an attitude of openness to learning from within and from the other participants around them.

Realm: This transmission proposes, in its model of a agapéic space, that there are 65,000 discrete levels of agapéic frequency. Each level is a realm that provides a possible location for a node of Dao-consciousness comprising spiritual identity, and typically, for a population of such nodes.

Religion: An informal or formalised organisation providing social engagement in a common interest. That interest is normally directed towards non-physical existence in order to contextualise human life.

Rena (shipwreck): The container ship Rena ran aground on the Astrolabe Reef near Tauranga, New Zealand, on 5 October, 2011.

Sensitivity: The ability to respond to stimuli or to register small differences in stimuli.

Sentience: The readiness to perceive sensations. Also indicates an elementary or undifferentiated consciousness.

Shag: A type of seabird.

Shiva: A Hindu god associated with reproduction and dissolution.

Sit: To sit in meditation, that is, to be physically still in a comfortable position and focus one's attention on the mental and/or spiritual domains of existence.

Soul (group): In undivided form, the node of Dao-consciousness. In divided form, a cluster of fragments, more commonly known as individual souls or spirits, each of which incarnates individually in order to gather information. At the end of the cycle of incarnations the fragments re-unite to form a mature and refined node of Dao-consciousness. This transmission comes from such a re-united group soul.

Soul (individual): One fragment of a node of Dao-consciousness manifesting as and comprising a spirit-sphere that co-associates and coalesces with a human animal body, thereby animating it.

Spirit: See *Soul* and *Spirit-sphere*.

Spirit-sphere: An individual fragment of a node of Dao-consciousness. In human beings it manifests at the hara-level structure and defines individual human identity. It may only be observed via non-physical visual perception using the auric channel.

Spiritual realm: The Dao, including all of manifest and unmanifest existence.

Spirituality: The idea or act of attending to a generally invisible domain of reality. Historically, it has been defined in different ways by different religions and cultures.

Survival: When a physical body dies its associated lower mind dies with it. What survives is the accumulated information gathered during incarnation, and the spiritual self and its higher mind to which that information is uploaded.

Teaching (spiritual): A knowledge-set deliberately transferred from identity in spirit to lower mind in body.

The Real: An historical spiritual conception that proposes that the spiritual domain is more significant and real than the physical domain. Neither distortion is supported in this teaching.

Time (disrupted or missing): Accessing the higher mind's level of awareness is normally associated with apparent disruptions or discontinuities in the ordinary awareness of passing time. This is a consequence of the functioning of bio-consciousness, not of Dao-consciousness.

Tinnitus: The perception of sound within the human ear or mind in the absence of corresponding external sound.

Trance: A condition in which attention is re-allocated away from normal alert conscious attending to physical life.

Transmission (spiritual): A spiritually initiated transfer from a higher mind to a lower mind, usually comprising knowledge of spiritual existence, of physical existence from a spiritual perspective, and the relations between them.

Vipassana: Ancient Buddhist technique of meditation designed to eliminate psychological complexes resulting from traumatic experience in both present and prior lives.

Yellowhammer: A type of finch (bird)

Index

www.ingramcontent.com/pod-product-compliance
Lightning Source LLC
Chambersburg PA
CBHW022202050726
47590CB00002B/615